NO MORE SITTING ON THE OLD SCHOOL BENCH

By Alan Bleasdale

DETENTION

By David Calcutt
edited by Ray Speakman

samuelfrench.co.uk

Copyright No More Sitting on the Old School Bench © Alan Bleasdale 1979
Detention© David Calcutt 1987, Editorial matter© Ray Speakman 1987
This selection© 1987, First published 1987, Reprinted 1988
All Rights Reserved

NO MORE SITTING ON THE OLD SCHOOL BENCH/ DETENTION is fully protected under the copyright laws of the British Commonwealth, including Canada, the United States of America, and all other countries of the Copyright Union. All rights, including professional and amateur stage productions, recitation, lecturing, public reading, motion picture, radio broadcasting, television and the rights of translation into foreign languages are strictly reserved.

ISBN 978-0-573-11691-9

www.samuelfrench.co.uk
www.samuelfrench.com

For Amateur Production Enquiries

UNITED KINGDOM AND WORLD
EXCLUDING NORTH AMERICA
plays@samuelfrench.co.uk
020 7255 4302/01

Each title is subject to availability from Samuel French, depending upon country of performance.

CAUTION: Professional and amateur producers are hereby warned that *NO MORE SITTING ON THE OLD SCHOOL BENCH/ DETENTION* is subject to a licensing fee. Publication of this play does not imply availability for performance. Both amateurs and professionals considering a production are strongly advised to apply to the appropriate agent before starting rehearsals, advertising, or booking a theatre. A licensing fee must be paid whether the title is presented for charity or gain and whether or not admission is charged.

The Professional Rights in this play are controlled by The Agency (London) Ltd, 24 Pottery Lane, Holland Park, London W11 4 LZ.

No one shall make any changes in this title for the purpose of production. No part of this book may be reproduced, stored in a retrieval system, or transmitted in any form, by any means, now known or yet to be invented, including mechanical, electronic, photocopying, recording, videotaping, or otherwise, without the prior written permission of the publisher. No one shall upload this title, or part of this title, to any social media websites.

The right of Alan Bleasdale and David Calcutt to be identified as authors of this work has been asserted in accordance with Section 77 of the Copyright, Designs and Patents Act 1988.

CONTENTS

Introduction   vii

NO MORE SITTING ON THE OLD SCHOOL BENCH
by Alan Bleasdale   1

DETENTION
by David Calcutt   93

Support and Resources   148

Introduction

'What I want to show is ... the life that isn't being lived, the people who could be fulfilled – and aren't.'

Alan Bleasdale said this in an interview with the *Radio Times* at the time of the first broadcast of *Boys From the Blackstuff* in 1982. That series of plays was probably the most memorable piece of television shown during this decade – 'a jewel in a soggy schedule', I think the *Observer* newspaper called it. Bleasdale might well have said the same of his recent stage play about Elvis Presley, *Are You Lonesome Tonight?* – or about his filmscript, *No Surrender* – passionate and powerful dramas dealing with wasted lives, and people who clearly have the capacity to give so much more than their circumstances and their surroundings allow.

No More Sitting on the Old School Bench and *Detention* by David Calcutt might well be introduced with the same remark. Bleasdale's pupils 'don't get nothin' unless you fight for it', his teachers, with their fears, doubts, evasions and clumsinesses, even the caretaker and his awful fascism, all show 'a life that isn't being lived'. Calcutt's school kids are shown to be frustrated and angered by teachers who do not know how to listen, and who have difficulty understanding what it is like 'to grow up here, and live here, and die here', and teachers who have become brutalised or who are confused about how to respond to the kids they teach. Life in both these schools 'isn't being lived', yet both writers show a collection of individuals who, for the most part, have an enormous potential and capacity – given a more honest approach and a society more aware of the damage it does to people in the inner city – there to be fulfilled. In *Detention* Blower's relationship with his grandfather and his defence of Makhan, Sarah's clear desire to listen and understand; in *No More Sitting on the Old School Bench* the kids' absolute disdain for the caretaker and his racist views, their perception and astringent humour, the teachers' untapped capacity to care for their pupils and each other despite the ineptitude and bickering which surrounds them – all point towards something like hope.

Introduction

Both plays are honest, complex and painfully accurate about some aspects of school which the teacher will surely recognise — as will students. That honesty and complexity (no easy answers or neat morals) is what makes them such good plays, and why they are presented here in a series to be used in schools. It is also why some teachers may find the plays unsettling and uncomfortable to read in the classroom. Teachers of English will recognise that what is seen as 'suitable' and entirely 'appropriate' for a theatre audience, or for performance by a Youth Theatre group, may well take a little more courage and preparation for use in the classroom. These are excellent plays, richly rewarding and stimulating, representative of the best contemporary drama, but they should be approached with care and within the context of a carefully thought out programme of classroom work.

The teacher will, of course, make a very basic choice about approach: as 'literature', in which case the discussion and writing undertaken by the group will turn the student back on the scripts themselves, or as a 'springboard' for more personal and anecdotal reflection and discussion upon the issues raised by the two plays. With the former approach both plays offer a rich variety of possible responses — from straightforward character exploration to a detailed examination of the plays' comments upon education, class and racism. The latter approach — a more personal and open-ended development of the situations and ideas in the plays — is a line of response best decided upon by the individual teacher in the light of his or her knowledge of, and ease with, a particular group of students.

The writers of these two plays neither disguise nor evade the issues raised by their subjects. Alan Bleasdale has described that section of society described in his play as 'like a kid with pebble glasses who's always being picked on'. The classroom teacher, similarly, ought not to be neutral about that 'kid with pebble glasses'. Discussion about issues (such as racism) may well expose attitudes which the teacher finds unacceptable. The plays expose those attitudes, and undermine them — so should the classroom teacher.

In view of all this, the teacher may well feel the need of

Introduction

support. A list of sources of support is given at the end of the collection, but I would also suggest that help from, and discussion with, colleagues in the English (or Drama) Department often provides excellent guidance — especially if that department has, or is developing, long-term policies on some of the issues raised in the plays. Multi-cultural support units also should be approached where possible for support and advice.

Given such care and preparation, these are the sort of plays that can change attitudes — not in a narrow party-political sense, but in terms of how we see each other and how we see ourselves.

RAY SPEAKMAN

Note: In some instances the language in Alan Bleasdale's play has been modified for classroom use in consultation with the author.

NO MORE SITTING ON THE OLD SCHOOL BENCH

First performed by the Contact Theatre Company at the University Theatre, Manchester, on 23 November 1977 with the following cast:

CARETAKER	Cliff Howells
CLEANER/TEA LADY/ FIRST GIRL	Julia Chambers
MISS McKENSIE	Sally Gibson
MRS SWIFT	Marlene Sidaway
MR DEAN	David Fleeshman
MR HADDOCK	Christopher Ravenscroft
MR WRIGHT	John Branwell
FIRST BOY	John Wheatley
MR GRANT	Nigel Bowden
PUPILS	Alan Bishop, Lorraine Bruce, David Cavanagh, Kevin Clinton, Gillian Coombes, Jennifer Cudjoe, Mike Durber, Jackie Harper, Caroline Kinsella, Chris Lyons, Stephen Mahr, Dawn Marchant, Sally de Meza, Joan Nisbett, Edwin Ogbogu, Sharon Raymond, Gurnam Singh, Kenneth Spence, Nadia Strachan, Ron Williams

Directed by CAROLINE SMITH
Designed by CAROL BETERA

CHARACTERS

CARETAKER, Mr Jackson
MISS McKENSIE, an elderly spinster and teacher
MRS SWIFT, Deputy Head
MR DEAN, Art teacher
MR HADDOCK, PE teacher
MR WRIGHT, new teacher of Sociology
MR GRANT, Headmaster
CLEANER
TEA LADY
A NEW BOY

Members of 5S
LURCH, Britton
FIRST BOY, Logmond
SECOND BOY
THIRD BOY
FOURTH BOY, Pembroke
LONER
WHITE BOY, Jimmy
FIRST GIRL, Jacqueline
SECOND GIRL, Helen
FIRST BLACK KID
SECOND BLACK KID
McKENNA

Other members of 5S and various school pupils

The play is set in the staffroom of a comprehensive school, somewhere in the North of England.

ACT ONE

(*Eight twenty-five in the morning, the first day of the autumn term. The wing of a large comprehensive school in a northern city.*)

(*We see the staffroom. Usual posters on the wall. NAS/NUT notices, a few tired framed photographs of 'The Old School', dead calendars illustrating the charitable works of the Seventh Day Adventists in Botswanaland. A notice board and a row of pigeon holes completely bare. Another row of small cupboards on the wall, full of exercise books, neatly stacked. Side stage right, by the door to the corridor, is a desk covered in mountains of more books and a duplicator with broken arm. There is a sign on it saying 'Broken'. Small window on the back wall, covered by a curtain. Centre stage, against the back wall, is a record player on a table, portable but large. LPs scattered on top of it and a large collection underneath. Directly above, and tilted at an angle, is a large Jubilee portrait of the Queen and the Duke of Edinburgh. Stage left, there are four easy chairs facing out, plus a coffee table. There is a staff pay telephone by the door.*)

(*The corridor, stage right, runs towards the audience.*)

(*We hear a Victor Sylvester record.*)

(*The lights come up.*)

(*We see the* CLEANER *dancing gently with her mop. Hardly moving, wistful.*)

(*We see the* CARETAKER *enter the corridor looking at his watch. Goes to walk past the staffroom. Sees the* CLEANER, *stands by the door. Coughs. She stops. Turns the record off. Starts mopping. He enters the room, touches up the Queen's portrait. As soon as he lets go it slips at an angle again. He begins pacing up and down. As he speaks, he goes* straight through the area that she is mopping. She does it again with a lack of interest that suggests that she is not over enamoured with her work.)

CARETAKER: ... seven weeks of peace ... gone, all gone ... seems like only yesterday it was the end of the summer term an' I was bolting the door on the little bastards ... (*Looks at his watch again*) ... another half an hour an' then ... (*Shivers*) ... there'll they be, droves of them at the door again, dead eyed an' dirty nosed, every single one of them straight out of the Village of the Damned ...

(*We see* MISS McKENSIE *come down the corridor and enter the staffroom. The* CARETAKER *looks at her, watches her walk towards the easy chairs. She is erect and proud looking but nods almost imperceptibly. He sneers quietly to himself.* MISS McKENSIE *walks right through the patch that the cleaner has been mopping. There is a record cover on her chair. She picks it up and places it on the coffee table. By this time the* CARETAKER *has returned to his packing.*)

CLEANER (*as she scrubs at something on the floor*): Someone in here last night, was there? (*She goes down on her hands and knees to inspect the marks*)
CARETAKER (*still striding and lost*): What? Who? Someone? No. (*Looks quickly across at* MISS McKENSIE, *who stares out*)
CLEANER: A meetin' like.
CARETAKER: No.
CLEANER: No?
CARETAKER: No.
CLEANER: Oh.
CARETAKER: And I would know. A caretaker living adjacent to the premises, such as myself, would be in a position to notice such things, would one not?
CLEANER: Well, there's a right mess over there that wasn't there yesterday afternoon. (*Points to the floor*)
CARETAKER: Really? Yes, well, still ... (*Looks across*) I'm sure you can get rid of it ... whatever it is. (*Smiles at her*)
CLEANER: Boot marks.

Act One

CARETAKER: Ah, boot marks. Oh.

CLEANER (*mimes out marching steps, looks up*): Y'can see f'y'self. Must have been someone.

CARETAKER: No, definitely not.

CLEANER (*basically disinterested*): Suit y'self, Mr Jackson.

CARETAKER: Well, then, there you are, you see. (*Looks at his watch, winces*) Right, yes. It won't be long now. (*Goes towards the door*) One way or another. (*He gets to the doorway. The phone rings*) I know who this'll be, certain. Miss Kite, sick again. It's bad news when y'have t'send the Schools Attendance Officer around to a member of staff. (*Picks up the phone. A good attempt at a formal educated voice*) Greenfields Comprehensive School, lower wing ... speak ... (*Change of voice*) Joey, what're ... (*Puts his hand over the mouthpiece. Looks around. The* CLEANER *is lighting a cigarette,* MISS McKENSIE *staring out*) ... what? In here ... last n— ... Oh Christ, you stupid ... bloody ... The very first time we have one on my patch and this happens ... (*He nearly has his lips down the phone*) ... what record was in the cover when you got home ... K-Tel's what? K-Tel's '20 Greatest Hymns' ... (*We see* MISS McKENSIE *glance down at the record*) ... yeah, all right, I'll look ... yeah, yeah, yeah ... 'sorry' ... sorry isn't good enough, Joey, not with a mistake like that.

(*He throws the phone down, turns, looks at the two women. He saunters towards the record player. Casually stands by the machine. Looks across again.* CLEANER *mopping, back turned,* MISS McKENSIE *as was. He picks up a couple of record sleeves, glances at them, puts them down. We see* MISS McKENSIE *look at him. He turns to look at her again. She looks out. He starts searching the other records, becoming more and more anxious and manic. Sleeves start spilling out onto the floor. The* CLEANER *looks up from her work. He looks around, she looks away. He carries on. Still more records fall. Both women look at him. As he turns towards them,* MISS McKENSIE *looks away, but the* CLEANER *stares at him.*)

CLEANER (*pause*): Lookin' for somethin', Mr Jackson?

CARETAKER: Who — me? No, no, just ... perusing ...

No More Sitting on the Old School Bench

(*He then sees* MISS McKENSIE *pick up the record sleeve off the coffee table. He sees that it is the one that he wants. Drops the other records, turns towards* MISS McKENSIE.)

CLEANER: There's some more Victor Sylvester there.

CARETAKER: Er, yes ... no doubt ...

CLEANER: No one's played them f'years. Except me.

CARETAKER: Not strictly allowed, of course, but ... (*He is trying to get away to* MISS McKENSIE)

CLEANER: It always relaxes me, listenin' t'Victor Sylvester.

CARETAKER: Ah ...

CLEANER: An' Henry Hall.

CARETAKER: Yes, Henry ...

CLEANER: Reminds me of the good old days ...

CARETAKER: Indeed, that's what we all like t'think about, now if ... (*Sees* MISS McKENSIE *taking the LP out of the sleeve*)

CLEANER: Me an' Harry down the *Locarno*, doin' the Palais Glide ...

CARETAKER (*moving away*): Why don't you, er ... (MISS McKEN-SIE *is inspecting the record*) Why don't you put the other side on, eh? (*She brightens, goes across to the record player as he advances on* MISS McKENSIE)

CLEANER: We were happy then ...

CARETAKER (*over his shoulder*): Yes, quite, quite ...

MISS McKENSIE: I know, oh yes, I know.

CARETAKER: What? Pardon? Know?

MISS McKENSIE: I've always known ... but nobody listens any more ...

CARETAKER (*goes to grab the record and the sleeve*): Let me ... (*She holds it away from him*) Let me put it back for you ...

(*She holds it above her head. He grabs it, the music starts, for a second they struggle like two demented dancing partners, then he snatches it away from her. The* CLEANER *turns on tiptoes. The* CARETAKER *comes away from* MISS McKENSIE, *she slowly puts her hands down. Sighs, then straightens up.*)

MISS McKENSIE: Marching ... marching again ...

Act One

(MRS SWIFT *enters the corridor carrying her timetable and foolscap duplicates of the timetable.*)

CLEANER: No, it's all foxtrots on this side ...
CARETAKER (*to the* CLEANER, *who is not listening*): Right, fine, found it! (*Holds the record up as he makes for the door*) The RI staff've been lookin' f'this f'weeks – er – months in fact. I'll just take it back to ...

(*He turns and bumps into* MRS SWIFT. *The edge of the board knocks against the record and it falls to the floor. He practically dives after it.*)

MRS SWIFT: Oh I am sorry ... I hope I haven't damanged it, Mr Jackson? (*Pause, as he tries to hide it behind his back*) Your personal collection?
CARETAKER (*hearty laugh*): No, no, no, good Lord no. (*Brings it out briefly from behind his back*)
MRS SWIFT: 'Twenty Greatest ...'?
CARETAKER: It was lost you see, and I found it.
MRS SWIFT: Jolly good for you.
CARETAKER (*half turns*): And I was just about to return it to the appropriate department.
MRS SWIFT: Oh no, I don't think I can let you do that.
CARETAKER (*pause*): Er ... why not?
MRS SWIFT (*cheerfully*): Well well well, and you've been here all these years, Mr Jackson, since the days when we were a tiny sleepy old grammar school, and you've forgotten that now we're a thriving dynamic fully integrated comprehensive school, the RI department's half a mile up the road in the main block.
CARETAKER: Er well, I just thought ... you know ... I'd rush ... they may well need it. Assembly ...
MRS SWIFT: Oh, I couldn't bear to think of you traipsing all the way up there on the very first morning ...
CARETAKER: Think nothing of it ...
MRS SWIFT (*as she takes the record off him*): ... Especially when I want you to go down to my office and get the master copy of

the new timetable off my desk. (*She smiles at him*) Oh, and the name of the new member of staff. (*Pause*) Thank you, Mr Jackson.

(*He reluctantly goes out of the door and off. All this time the music has been playing.* MRS SWIFT *looks around the staffroom, looks at the* CLEANER *as she walks across to the record player.*)

MRS SWIFT: Music while you work?

CLEANER: Er ... oh ... oh yes. (*She turns the record player off as* MRS SWIFT *puts the* CARETAKER's *record on the top of the machine*) I was just ... I've finished now, Mrs Swift ... (*She picks up her mop and bucket,* MRS SWIFT *smiles genuinely at her. She goes*)

(*At this point* MRS SWIFT *is radiating control, composure and confidence. She turns and looks across at* MISS McKENSIE. *Hesitates, seems as if she is gathering her strength to talk to* MISS McKENSIE.)

MRS SWIFT: Hello Maisie, have a good holiday? What was it again – somewhere exotic, wasn't it? (*Pause*) Everything go all right?

MISS McKENSIE (*as she nods*): No, not really. My friend was ill.

MRS SWIFT: Miss Stewart from Belle Vale ... Rose?

MISS McKENSIE: Very ill.

MRS SWIFT: I am sorry. I knew she wasn't in the best of health. (*Pause*) But apart from that, you know ...

MISS McKENSIE: There was nothing else apart from that. You see, she's dead.

MRS SWIFT: Oh! Oh Maisie, I really ...

MISS McKENSIE: No ...

MRS SWIFT: But you were so ... close.

MISS McKENSIE: I'd expected it.

MRS SWIFT: But your holiday ...

MISS McKENSIE: A holiday of a lifetime. (*She laughs*)

MRS SWIFT: You'd planned it for so long ...

MISS McKENSIE: She couldn't go. (*Pause*) Not because she was dead, you understand. She wasn't dead then.

MRS SWIFT: If there's anything I can do, you know that, please ...
MISS McKENSIE: You can listen to me ... (*She looks at* MRS SWIFT)
MRS SWIFT: Yes, go on.
MISS McKENSIE: It's about the caretaker ...
MRS SWIFT: Oh no, Maisie, not again. Please.
MISS McKENSIE (*leans back in her chair*): You don't believe me, do you? (*Pause*)
MRS SWIFT: It's not a question of believing Maisie, its a question of having ...
MISS McKENSIE: But I have proof now. (*Glances across at the record player*)
MRS SWIFT: Tell me, Maisie. (*A tone of voice used with her pupils*)
MISS McKENSIE: But you'll not believe me even now. (*Pause*) I'll just have to show you, won't I?
MRS SWIFT: If there is anything else I can do, if you need company ...
MISS McKENSIE: I've bought a dog. (*Looks at* MRS SWIFT) To keep me company.
MRS SWIFT: I suppose it will help ...
MISS McKENSIE: It's a big dog.
MRS SWIFT: Yes ... and the new term starting. Time will fly ...
MISS McKENSIE (*as* MR DEAN *walks down the corridor. She takes hold of* MRS SWIFT's *arm*): But we hardly have any time left.
MRS SWIFT (*as she takes her arm away*): Yes, Maisie. Yes.

(MR DEAN *enters. Smart jeans, polo neck pullover, expensive leather jacket, art folder,* Guardian *newspaper in his other hand. Agitated.*)

MR DEAN (*holding the* Guardian *up as he puts his art folder down by the pigeon holes*): What about this, Mrs Swift? Have you seen this? (*As* MRS SWIFT *moves away from* MISS McKENSIE) The *Guardian* this morning!
MRS SWIFT (*mocking him gently*): Oh, it hasn't gone up again, has it?
MR DEAN: The Education Authority! Don't you know what the Committee's done?
MRS SWIFT: Learnt to read?
MR DEAN: They can't do it!

MRS SWIFT: No, probably not.

MR DEAN (*listening at last*): Oh come on, Mrs Swift, this is no time for jokes.

MRS SWIFT: The start of term is the only time for jokes, Mr Dean.

MR DEAN: Well, I don't think you'll be laughing after you read this, I really don't. (*He sees that she is smiling*) Oh now, come on, I'm sorry, but as NUT representative, I find it singularly unfunny.

MRS SWIFT: But what do you find it as a human being?

MR DEAN: Oh, don't be so patronising, Freda ... oh look, look for yourself. (*He hands her the paper. She looks at the paper*) Morning Maisie, have you heard? (*She nods. Normally even he would realise that her nodding is no acknowledgement, but he carries on oblivious*) Yes, by Christ, it's not good, is it? Another sign of the times, all right. The move to the right, hah! (*He starts pacing up and down the room in a similar fashion to the* CARETAKER *earlier*) Anyway ... have a nice holiday?

MISS McKENSIE: No.

MR DEAN: Good, good. There'll be trouble over this, I'm telling you, trouble. It could well break up any union solidarity that there is. Can you imagine the wheeling and dealing that's going to take place now, the sucking up and sneakiness, every man for himself, the tension in the staffroom – everyone looking at each other and wondering, 'Is it him? Or is it me?' It won't do us any good at all ...

MRS SWIFT (*handing the paper back*): It might even have an effect on the children.

MR DEAN: Oh now, come on, Freda, you know I've always put the needs and consideration of ...

MRS SWIFT (*putting her hand up, stopping him in mid-rhetoric*): Indeed you have.

MR DEAN: I'm glad that ...

MRS SWIFT (*advancing on him*): In fact, there's many a time I've felt like wrapping you up and taking you home, spilling you on the carpet in front of my husband and saying, 'There you are, Eric, look, see, that's the one I was telling you about, that was you and me fifteen years ago, except we wore duffle coats and scarves and marched for peace ...'

Act One

MR DEAN: You?

MRS SWIFT: Me.

MR DEAN: You marched? Aldermaston to . . .

MRS SWIFT: Part of the way.

MR DEAN: What went wrong?

MRS SWIFT: 'What went wrong?' Nothing went wrong, Graham. Everything went right. We both got promotion, a bigger house in a better area, two cars and a deep freeze. (*She smiles at him. Goes towards the pigeon holes*)

MISS McKENSIE: I've just bought a dog.

MR DEAN (*not quite certain who to talk to*): Yes, really? (*She nods, and he then directs his conversation towards* MRS SWIFT) Well, I er, I don't know what that's got to do with this. (*Waves the paper at* MRS SWIFT)

MISS McKENSIE: I could have bought a car.

MR DEAN: No, I meant . . . (*Indicates* MRS SWIFT, *then his newspaper*)

MISS McKENSIE: But I can't drive. (*She motions towards him*) Come here. I want to tell you something.

MR DEAN: Not just now, Maisie. (*He waves the paper*) You know . . .

(*He walks away. She watches him go, then stands, begins to walk across to the record player.* MRS SWIFT *watches as* DEAN *comes towards her.* MISS McKENSIE *picks up '20 Greatest Hymns' cover.*)

MRS SWIFT: Maisie, are you . . . you know, are you . . .

MISS McKENSIE: I left my bag in the . . .

MRS SWIFT (*as* MISS McKENSIE *looks at the record*): No, I mean, if it's too much . . .

MISS McKENSIE: I can do what needs to be done on my own. (*She puts the record back in the cover. Half smiles. Takes the record with her*)

MRS SWIFT: Anything at all, please don't be afraid.

MISS McKENSIE: If you know of anyone who could look after my dog?

(*She goes out.* MR DEAN *looks questioningly at* MRS SWIFT.)

MRS SWIFT: Her friend has died.

MR DEAN: Miss Stewart? (MRS SWIFT *nods. She has finished putting the timetables in the pigeon holes. She hands him his*) How terribly sad. (*Looks towards the door, then turns back, brandishes the paper*) But what I can't understand is how you can be so matter of fact about it all. I quite frankly couldn't believe it when I first ...

MRS SWIFT: I'm afraid I knew at the end of the summer term.

MR DEAN: *What?*

MRS SWIFT (*walking away from him towards the door*): Poor Maisie. I always said it wouldn't take much of a push ... and such a good teacher ... once ... you should have seen her, you would have liked her, Graham, she shared your ...

MR DEAN: You're avoiding the issue, Mrs Swift.

MRS SWIFT: Yes, I know. (*She walks away from the door towards the chairs*)

MR DEAN (*as he follows her*): We had a right to be told about this. (*Waves the paper again*) And to be told as soon as the hierarchy in the school knew.

MRS SWIFT: On the last day of term? (*He nods*) What did you want me to say? 'Oh, and by the way, now that we are all gathered together, apart from the headmaster, who has once again managed to lock himself in his cloakroom, I would just like to mention that at the end of the Autumn term we will be nominating two of you for transfer to another unspecified understaffed school, under the Education Authority's new redeployment scheme ...'

MR DEAN: But ...

MRS SWIFT: 'You will have no choice in the matter, other than resignation and almost inevitable unemployment, because it is highly likely that we will select those two members of staff who are either useless or lazy, continually sick, troublemakers, socialists or soft enough to go without a fight. Have a pleasant holiday.'

MR DEAN: There's ways and bloody means.

MRS SWIFT: Not with an ultimatum as precise as this one.

MR DEAN: So it is definite?

MRS SWIFT: Your union ...

Act One

MR DEAN (*quickly*): The same union as yours.

> (MR HADDOCK *enters, unnoticed for some time (until he speaks). Wearing a sports jacket, flannels and sun tan, carrying an 'Adidas' bag. Stands at the doorway, listening.*)

MRS SWIFT: But more yours than mine. (*Takes the newspaper*) 'The teachers' union hammered out the redeployment agreement with the Education Authorities over six months ago ...'

MR DEAN: Nobody told me.

MRS SWIFT: Don't you know, Graham, there's even hierarchies in trade unions? (*Looks down at the paper again*) ... 'over six months ago in a bid by both sides to avoid redundancies in schools that are overstaffed.' Supposedly overstaffed. (*She looks up*) Morning, Donald. Glad to be back? (*He scowls at her*)

MR DEAN (*ignoring* HADDOCK): It was voluntary. They asked for volunteers, that's all I heard. Nobody said ...

MRS SWIFT: And surprise, surprise, they got not a one.

MR HADDOCK: And you know why, don't you? Because the only schools that are understaffed are the slum schools. Full of slum kids and slum attitudes. And slum teachers. Martyrs and misfits.

MR DEAN: Yeah, that's just the kind of attitude I would have expected from you.

MR HADDOCK: You mean that it's typically sensible, shrewd and down to earth?

MR DEAN: The adjective I was thinking of was 'ignorant'. And if you must know, Haddock, my definition of a slum school would include this school, and the attitudes of some of its teachers.

MR HADDOCK: Definitions hey? (*To* MRS SWIFT) Dean's Walking Oxford Dictionary.

MR DEAN: The fact is that the system is created by those who work within it. It's the people who are at fault. People like you.

MR HADDOCK: And that's where you're wrong, Che baby. The fault is the system.

MRS SWIFT: Oh, here we go again ...

MR DEAN: Absolute rubbish. You don't know what you're talking about. If the system's wrong. It's up to us to put it right. (HADDOCK *yawns at him*) Although if it was up to you, nothing'd ever get done. Except press-ups.

MR HADDOCK: Poor Graham, if only ideals were realities ... Listen sunbeam, systems are the wonderful ideas of wonderful people in their ivory education offices and cabinet meetings – and when it comes down to us, to Mr and Mrs Joe Rabble, we can't put them into practice – and you know why – because we're not wonderful people with wonderful minds – because the kids and their parents aren't wonderful people – because in our case our headmaster is a wonderful wet ... (*We see the* NEW BOY *approach from the corridor, stand at the door to the staffroom, hesitate, then knock*) ... and because it isn't a wonderful world outside the corridors of power. (HADDOCK *moves towards the door*) And I'll tell you something now ... you – you can't change anything, pal.

MR DEAN: Ah, shit Haddock! (*As* HADDOCK *opens the door and the* NEW BOY *sees and hears* MR DEAN) I mean ...

MR HADDOCK (*pointing to* DEAN): That's the one, he said it, son. He's the Art Teacher you see, and Art Teachers can say and do anything on account of their artistic temperaments. (*Brings the boy into the room*) Now then, yes, what can we do for you? Been beaten up already, have you? Knifed for your dinner money at the school gates? (MRS SWIFT *moves across*)

NEW BOY: Please Sir, I'm los— ...

MR HADDOCK: Out boy, out!

(*The boy fidgets, looks on the point of tears.* MRS SWIFT *looks at* MR HADDOCK *angrily, takes hold of the boy's arm and leads him out.*)

MRS SWIFT: Now, I think you're a trifle early, and if I were you, I would go and wait in the playground. (*She takes him up the corridor*)

MR HADDOCK (*shouts after the boy*): And just in case you grow up to be a future pupil governor of this school, I'd like you to know that language like that deeply offends my sensibilities ...

(MRS SWIFT *points away to stage right, and the boy goes off*)

MR DEAN: You have such a way with children, Haddock, I've

always admired you for that. (*He turns away.* MRS SWIFT *enters the room, closes the door*)

MRS SWIFT: Now there's someone who'll always remember his first day at this school. (HADDOCK *ignores her, walks towards the chairs, sits down*)

MR HADDOCK: All the first years will remember it. Who else but our glorious headmaster would have a whole wing composed purely of first-year pupils and fifth-form terrorists.

MR DEAN (*indicates the paper*): Anyway, they just can't do it ...

MRS SWIFT: Oh Christ, Graham! (*Calmer*) Look, 'they' can and 'they' will.

MR DEAN: And you're going to be one of them.

MR HADDOCK: I'm sure that our beloved headmaster will seek Freda's advice.

MR DEAN (*without looking at* HADDOCK): And ask her to make the decision.

MR HADDOCK: Before informing the unlucky contestants.

MRS SWIFT: Oh, now stop it, you two ...

MR DEAN: Yeah, well, we'll see about that.

MR HADDOCK: Like you were going to see about the local authorities' proposal to reinstate the eleven plus?

MR DEAN: We at least brought it to the public's attention. The debate that followed, the one-day strikes ... (*Looks at them*) ... you ... you just can't do *nothing*.

MR HADDOCK (*yawning*): Oh yes you can. And very easily too.

MR DEAN: Jesus. I hope I never end up like you two.

MR HADDOCK: Oooh! Careful now. That alone may well have moved you a couple of places up the redeployment list ...

MR DEAN: Ah shut up, Haddock, you know nothing. (*To* MRS SWIFT) Until I told him, he thought the millennium was a picture house in town.

MR HADDOCK: Hah hah bloody hah. And the state of you, arty-farty, weak as weasel's piss, couldn't even chase the paint when it runs. (*They stare at each other*) Took a football team for me once, you know. Thought the left winger was a member of the Communist Party.

MRS SWIFT (*at the ceiling, and tired*): Oh, it's so reassuring, on the first day of term, to find that nothing's changed. (*Pause, then an attempt at deflation*) If you really want to fight, gentlemen, I suggest you go behind the toilets in the boys' playground, that's the normal custom in this school.

MR DEAN (*walking towards the door*): Well anyway, Mrs Swift, I'd be grateful if you would add to the Staff Notices that a union meeting will take place at four o'clock in A5. And that's not just for this staffroom, but also the Main School. (HADDOCK hums 'The Red Flag' in the background) Could you please mark it 'most urgent'?

MRS SWIFT: I'll mention it to the secretary.

MR DEAN: Won't be much use, will it? You know as well as I do that the secretary arrives with the Headmaster, which means that they will both be late.

MRS SWIFT: You could always make the addition to the staff notices yourself, seeing as you feel so strongly about it.

MR DEAN: I have some phone calls to make.

MRS SWIFT: Planning union strategy?

(*Outside, in the corridor, we see a black lad approach the door. Big, Afro hairstyle, looking around to make sure no one can see him.*)

MR DEAN: Of course.

MRS SWIFT: I just love you when you're being terribly, terribly formal, Graham. You really are ever so cute. (*Another smile. He opens his mouth — no words. Snorts, goes towards the door as the boy knocks on it*) You'll find out, you can't fight fixed minds.

MR DEAN: Or constipated ones. (*He turns and opens the door, sees the boy as the* CARETAKER *comes into the corridor with the master timetable. He sees the boy*) Lurch! What are you doing up at this time of the morning?

LURCH: Well, it's like this, y'see, Sir ... (*Puts his hand in his jacket*)

CARETAKER: *You!* How did you get in here? Go on, get out, right now, come on ...

LURCH: But I only ...

CARETAKER: I hope for your sake I don't find any broken windows when I go on my rounds, that's ...

MR DEAN: Mr Jackson ...

Act One

CARETAKER: Let's be havin' y' ... disturbin' the teachers, enterin' the school ...

MR DEAN: If you don't mind ...

CARETAKER: But I do mind. This ... this pupil must have broken in, Mr Dean an' ...

LURCH: No I never, I never, this little kid opened the door from the inside an' ...

CARETAKER: An' pigs were seen flyin' around the playground, come on ... (*Grabs hold of* LURCH's *arm*)

LURCH: Let go, you! (*Pulls away.* MRS SWIFT *walks to the door.* MR DEAN *comes between the* CARETAKER *and* LURCH)

MR DEAN: The boy's telling the truth, Mr Jackson, and whether you mind it or not, I'll handle this.

CARETAKER: The school's my responsibility ...

MRS SWIFT: And I'll have the timetable, thank you, Mr Jackson.

CARETAKER: Yes, well, fine thing if we were overrun with kids at this time of the mornin'. You'd all be cursin' me then, wouldn't you? I'm only doin' my job y'know.

MRS SWIFT: And a fine job you make of it. Now could I have the timetable, please. (*The* CARETAKER *looks over* MRS SWIFT's *shoulder into the staffroom, edges into the room*)

CARETAKER: I'll put it on for you, Mrs Swift, I've brought some drawing pins ... and I've got the name of the new teacher as well ... (*He goes towards the record player and timetable board, already looking for the record*) Won't take long ...

MRS SWIFT: That will be quite all right, Mr Jackson. I can do that myself.

(*Pause. He looks for the record with anxiety.*)

Thank you again, Mr Jackson.

MR DEAN (*to* LURCH *as they walk down the corridor towards the auditorium*): Well then, what is it, lad?

LURCH (*embarrassed*): Y'know last term, Sir, when you were goin' on about the Art Gallery an' all that, an' y'said we should go. Remember? (DEAN *nods*) Yeah, well, me an' Johnno went. It was smart like y'said it would be. An' like, when I got home, I did this paintin' an' I wanted y' t'have a look at it ...

MR DEAN: Bring it in an' I'll certainly have a look at it.
LURCH (*bringing out a folded up painting of a still life from his jacket*): I brought it with me. (*Opens it out*)
MR DEAN: You know, it's not very good for a painting to be folded up into four.
LURCH (*as they go off*): I didn't want the others t'see me with it. Y'know what they say around our way – if y'a painter y'a puff unless y'emulsion walls . . .
MR DEAN: Hey, this is really good, Lurch. Come on, let's go and pin it up . . .

(*As this scene above develops, we see the* CARETAKER *reluctantly give the timetable to* MRS SWIFT, *go back to the door and look around. He sees that she is still watching him. He hurries into the corridor, looks angrily at* DEAN *and the boy, hurries away.* MRS SWIFT *pins the timetable on the board.*)

MRS SWIFT: Have a good holiday, Donald? (*She approaches with a timetable sheet*)
MR HADDOCK: Too good to come back here. (MRS SWIFT *gives him his sheet*) Do you have to, Freda? (*Drops it on the coffee table*) I mean, now I've dropped History completely, it hardly matters who I'll be taking, and I do know where I'm likely to be – in the gymnasium, or, if the weather's fine, I'll be on the field.
MRS SWIFT (*lightly*): Sitting underneath a tree, reading a motor magazine.
MR HADDOCK: Not always, I sometimes take *Sports Illustrated* out with me. (*She fails to smile*) Oh I see, I'm getting a little hint, am I? A motherly warning, a school Mam's reprimand, 'Try a little harder now, Donald dear, we don't want to have to redeploy you, do we?' (*He pushes back against the chair in mock horror*) 'Oh no, not redeployment, oh no, please, anything but that . . .'
MRS SWIFT: I'm just giving you your timetable, that's all.
MR HADDOCK: Yeah, what a pity you couldn't have given me the Head of PE last year. Perhaps then I might have . . .
MRS SWIFT: Now now, that wasn't my idea – or my decision.
MR HADDOCK: Well, don't tell me it was the Head's. Jesus,

getting any decision out of the Boss is like nailing jelly to the wall. (*Pause*) Why didn't I get the job? (*Pause*) I've been here a lot longer than Matthews. Why did he get it? (*Pause. He stands*) All right, all right Freda, a diplomatic silence, just what I would expect from you. I know why I didn't get the job. He's twenty-seven and I'm thirty-eight. I was his age once, I did it too, I had the energy and the bloody zeal ... but he'll learn, Matthews, so will Graham Dean, they'll find out. The only rewards you get in this job are twelve weeks' holiday a year and sugar in your petrol tank. You know that.

MRS SWIFT: Not entirely, Don; but I can understand the feeling.

MR HADDOCK: Course you can. But try telling them, the younger ones.

MRS SWIFT: Best not to know ...

MR HADDOCK: They make me laugh, they really do – they're always the same at the start of term, full of high ideals and surplus energy. Give them a few weeks of screaming kids and dinner duties, detentions and Miss Kite's perpetual sick notes losing them every free period they've ever had, and they'll only have one object left in life – how to survive till Christmas. (*We see* MR WRIGHT *and* MR DEAN *walking up the corridor towards the staffroom*) I tell you, there's nothing worse than being away from kids to make you forget what bastards they really are, and there's nothing more pathetic than trying to save a world that doesn't want to be saved.

(*The door opens with a flourish.* MR WRIGHT *enters with a flourish,* MR DEAN *close behind him.* MR WRIGHT *is a walking visual aid: roll of posters under one arm, a briefcase and an art folder. He carries them about with him throughout the first act.*)

MR WRIGHT: Good morning, good morning!

MR HADDOCK: Avon calling ...

MR DEAN: This is er ... I just found him looking a trifle lost; in fact getting chased through the quad by this massive bloody Alsatian ...

MRS SWIFT: Oh no, not dogs in the school already. (*She goes across towards* MR WRIGHT) You'll be er ... Mr ... (*She reaches the timetable where* JACKSON *has left the sheet containing the new teacher's name*)

MR WRIGHT: Wright.

MRS SWIFT: Mr Wright.

MR WRIGHT: That's right! Wright. Ronald Wright.

MRS SWIFT: Our new member of staff.

MR WRIGHT: Right! Or should I say correct?

MR HADDOCK (*walking away*): Won't last long.

MR DEAN: Don't start, Haddock ...

MR WRIGHT: Yes, it can get very confusing. I was recently teaching my youngest son the difference between right and left, and when I asked him to indicate his left hand, for example, and he pointed to his left, I said, 'That's right!' (*Pause*) You see. Right meaning *correct*, but he thought it was his right hand, when in reality it was his left. (*Pause. He looks around the room.* HADDOCK, *now seated with a motor magazine, peeps over the top of the cover*)

MRS SWIFT: Ah, how fascinating. Now, let me introduce you to ... (*She looks around at* HADDOCK, *who puts his magazine over his face*) ... Mr Dean, our Art Master, who ...

MR WRIGHT: Ah, Art, what an exhilarating subject. I have, myself, for many years, dabbled somewhat in oils, purely on an amateur level, for my own enjoyment ...

MR DEAN: That's what it's about, isn't it? Your own enjoyment.

MR WRIGHT: Of course. A fine attitude, one I'm sure you must bring to your teaching.

MR HADDOCK: He paints flags. Red ones.

MR WRIGHT: It was, I believe, Ted Hughes, the *Socialist* poet, who said, 'A great proportion of people have some artistic talent. It mightn't be much, but even the tiniest spark is very important to the person who has it.'

MRS SWIFT: Ah ...

MR HADDOCK (*quietly*): Urgh ...

MR DEAN (*quickly*): Very impressive.

MR WRIGHT: I have a photographic memory.

MR DEAN: No, I er ... meant the Ted Hughes quote.

Act One

MR WRIGHT: Oh. There was more to it, actually. Erm, let me see ...
MRS SWIFT (*moving him towards the easy chairs*): Mr Haddock, who is in charge of PE here in the wing ...
MR HADDOCK: If not throughout the school ... how do you do.
MR WRIGHT: Pleased to meet you. I did seriously consider doing PE at college as my main course, quite a sportsman in my time, you know, as you can probably tell, it never leaves you does it? But I was finally persuaded otherwise, age really, and my academic inclinations.
MR HADDOCK: What a loss to the gymnasium you must have been.
MR WRIGHT: Yes, I know, but I am still very interested, and I follow all the latest developments, of course. The whole concept of physical education has undergone quite a radical revolution in the last ten years, hasn't it? (DEAN *laughs*)
MR HADDOCK: It hasn't here.
MR WRIGHT: Yes, well naturally, some people are less adaptable to change, aren't they? (*Silence, apart from DEAN trying to suppress a giggle*) I mean, you know ... I'm not saying that change is altogether the perfect answer, the er solution to all the educational problems, but ...
MRS SWIFT (*taking hold of his arm*): Oh I do agree, Mr Wright. Obviously a subject for continued discussion — at some later date. Now, here is your timetable, I think it's fairly self-explanatory, although there might be a problem over your room, Room 12 (*Looks at the others*) but if there's anything you're not sure about, don't hesitate to ask me.
MR WRIGHT: Ah, I see, you're the secretary, I was wondering ...
MRS SWIFT: Erm, no, not quite, I'm the deputy headmistress, for my sins ...
MR WRIGHT: Oh, I do beg your pardon, Miss ... er, I don't know your ...
MRS SWIFT: *Mrs* Swift, and think nothing of it.
MR WRIGHT: I've only met the Headmaster.
MRS SWIFT: Yes, I was on a course when the interviews took place. Unfortunately.

MR WRIGHT: A very impressive man.

MR DEAN: Do you think so?

MR WRIGHT: Oh yes, fully in support of the modern methods, you know. Told me so himself.

MR DEAN: We rarely see him down here, so we wouldn't know.

MRS SWIFT (*as* WRIGHT *looks puzzled*): The Headmaster er ... functions from the main school, though he does pop over from time to time ...

MR HADDOCK: You know, to see the dregs, the cast-offs and cripples hidden away in the wing, out of the way, or perhaps a quick dash across to try and piece the timetable together, hey, Freda?

MRS SWIFT (*ignoring* HADDOCK): He will be here for Assembly this morning.

MR WRIGHT (*ignoring all*): There were 143 applicants for my position, you know. 143.

MR HADDOCK: And the Headmaster chose you.

MR WRIGHT: I was very lucky.

MRS SWIFT (*looks him up and down*): Yes, remarkably so.

MR DEAN: Of course, it's so difficult getting an appointment these days ...

MR WRIGHT: Especially your first one.

MR DEAN (*to* MRS SWIFT): And that's another reason why this redeployment issue is so ... (*Turns back*) ... did you say this is your *first* job?

MR WRIGHT: Absolutely.

MR HADDOCK (*politely, from behind his magazine*): Since you left school?

MR WRIGHT (*laughs*): Well, hardly, I was the manager of a wallpaper shop for many years, until there came a day when I realised that my life was spiritually ...

MRS SWIFT (*quickly*): So you left college this summer, then, Mr Wright?

MR WRIGHT: Ronald.

MRS SWIFT: Ronald.

MR WRIGHT: I do so dislike formality, don't you? (*Pause*)

MRS SWIFT: You left college this summer? Ronald.

Act One

MR WRIGHT (*for the first time reluctant*): The previous summer, as a matter of fact. I'd almost given up hope actually.

MR HADDOCK (*from behind his magazine*): I'm not surprised.

MR WRIGHT: Pardon?

MR HADDOCK: Er, I'm not surprised you er ... had difficulties. Straight out of college at this period in the er economic climate, as it were ...

MR WRIGHT: Exactly! It has been quite terrible.

MRS SWIFT: Shocking. Now, just one word of warning about this class ... (*She holds up the timetable*)

MR WRIGHT: I'd never even had an interview until I came here, and I'd applied for literally hundreds of ...

MRS SWIFT: Well, congratulations, here you are, but just let me tell you about ...

MR WRIGHT: My mistake was applying for senior positions.

MRS SWIFT: Ye— ... *senior* positions?

MR WRIGHT: Yes.

MR HADDOCK: They are so terribly reluctant to give headships to first-year teachers these days.

MR WRIGHT: I never actually applied for headships, well, apart from one for a Junior school in Huddersfield. Heads of Departments mainly. Year masters, such like. (*The others stare at him*) I have a degree in Education, you see.

MR HADDOCK: Ah, now you're talking. A degree, well, I mean, that explains everything, doesn't it? These days they give degrees away like loss-leaders at Tesco's. (*He gets progressively more worked up as he continues*) Us lesser mortals who merely went to training colleges in the fifties had to put up with old army barracks, a teachers' certificate, bromide in the tea and a quick bash behind the bushes of a Saturday night. Now, of course, it's all different, isn't it? Any fool with a felt-tip pen can get a degree in Education, and then, notwithstanding any ceremony, strip down to his pimply little juvenile bum and have it away in the middle of a lecture on Pavlov's performing dogs. (*He picks up his sports bag and moves towards the door*)

MR WRIGHT: I think the younger generation has a lot to offer.

MR HADDOCK: Oh Jesus Christ! If there's one thing that gets up my nose more than a young idealist, it's an old one. (*He storms out*)

MR WRIGHT: I do hope I haven't upset him.

MR DEAN: Take no notice of Mr Haddock, he's going through the first painful stages of the male menopause.

MRS SWIFT: In fact, take no notice of any of us, Mr Wright, Ronald. We're all on edge, you know, first day back, and one or two problems. (*She looks at* DEAN)

MR WRIGHT: I'm looking forward to it immensely.

MRS SWIFT (*pause*): Good for you, Ronald.

MR DEAN: Right ... (*Goes towards the door*)

MR WRIGHT: Ronald Wright!

MR DEAN: Er ... no, I er ... I'll leave you to it. (*Looks at* MRS SWIFT) I've got a lot to do. I never did get around to making those phone calls.

MRS SWIFT: Don't be too hasty organising, Graham, early days yet.

MR DEAN: Never too early.

MRS SWIFT: To start trouble?

MR DEAN: To organise.

MRS SWIFT: Strike action?

MR DEAN: If I have anything to do with it, yes. (*She shakes her head*) Look, Freda, you know as well as I do that it'll be two of us here that'll go. For a start the authority'd probably like nothing better than to close this place down – or start it up again, God forbid, as a grammar school!

MR WRIGHT: May I ask what is happening?

MR DEAN (*glances at* MRS SWIFT): Ah ... because the school is supposed to be overcrowded, staffwise, the education authority are going to forcibly move two teachers to another school at Christmas. It's called redeployment, a similar kind of word to resettlement.

MRS SWIFT: Graham, just ...

MR WRIGHT: But ... but if it's overstaffed, why am I here?

MRS SWIFT: We lost four members of staff in summer, and you were the only replacement. With your subject, Sociology, being a specialised subject, we had to have someone ...

MR WRIGHT: That's disgraceful, it really is. You can count on my full support.
MR DEAN: Er, right . . . good, great . . . (*Goes out quickly*)
MRS SWIFT: If you'll excuse me for a few moments, Mr Wright . . . Ronald, there are a number of things that need attending to, the first-year arrivals, registers, staff absences, such like, you understand . . . (*Moves to the door*)
MR WRIGHT: Can I be of any assistance? I do enjoy administration.
MRS SWIFT: Don't you think you'll have enough on your plate today . . . your first . . .
MR WRIGHT: I did very well on teaching practice.
MRS SWIFT (*firmly*): Be that as it may, I would be happier if you just sat down and studied your timetable; you know, get one or two things sorted out for yourself. The Headmaster has seen fit to give you a couple of . . . difficult classes, and the more prepared you are the better. Don't you agree? I won't be long. I'll show you your classroom before registration.
MR WRIGHT: Room 12.
MRS SWIFT (*winces*): Yes, Room 12.
MR WRIGHT: I remembered. My photographic memory.
MRS SWIFT: Indeed.

(*The* CARETAKER *enters the corridor, sneaks towards the door carrying a broom.*)

MR WRIGHT: I would like to see my room, if it's not too much . . .
MRS SWIFT: Time enough to see Room 12, just relax, Ronald. I'll be with you before the bell.

(*She goes towards the door, opens it. The* CARETAKER *dodges away from the door, pretends to sweep the corridor. We also hear banging from behind the emergency doors, front stage right. Cries of 'Why are we waiting' and 'There's going to be a riot.'*)

CARETAKER (*pointing off*): They're back again. Listen to them. Don't you worry, I'll soon sort them out.

(*Goes to walk towards the doors,* MRS SWIFT *walks towards the other end of the corridor. He stops and watches her go. Comes back, peeps around the edge of the door.* WRIGHT *is walking up and down, talking to himself, but not in a nervous manner. This man believes in himself.*)

MR WRIGHT: 'Good morning, I am your new sociology teacher, my name is Mr Wright ... Good morning, my name is Mister Wright, I am ... Good morning boys and girls ... hello there, boys and girls ... hiya kids, my name's Mr Wright, but I'm not one for formality, so go right ahead and call me Ronald ... Good morning ... Good morning ... (WRIGHT *turns and sees the* CARETAKER) Good morning.

CARETAKER: Mornin'. (*Makes sure no one else is there. Enters the room*)

MR WRIGHT: I am the new sociology master, Mr Wright. How do you do?

CARETAKER: Mr Jackson, caretaker.

MR WRIGHT (*looking at the broom*): I thought you might be. (*Pause as* JACKSON *edges towards the record player once again*) Do you happen to know where Room 12 is?

CARETAKER: Room 12. Oh yes, the new ones always get Room 12. (*A grim laugh*) It occupies an interesting position, does Room 12. Above the boiler room, next door to the Gym and at the side of the metalwork room. (*He has his back to the record player*) Sociology, did you say? You'll be replacing Miss Labbe, won't be missed that one, two ton of make-up an' never wore a bra. Had no cause to, if you ask me, but that's beside the point.

MR WRIGHT: I don't really want to talk about my predec—

CARETAKER: The point is, how can you learn sociology from someone who wore a cheesecloth top an' nothin' t'support her tits? 'Ey? What educational standards can you hope t'achieve when you don't wear a bra? Doesn't make sense at all.

MR WRIGHT: Can I just say ...

CARETAKER: I can remember this school when it was a grammar school, friend, when the staff all wore elbow patches, herringbone jackets an' smoked pipes. They looked like teachers, they thought like teachers an' they behaved like teachers. They read the *Daily Telegraph*, believed in the Commonwealth, drove Morris Minors an' spent their holidays in the Lake District. An' that was right! (*He reaches the record player, turns away from* WRIGHT)

MR WRIGHT: That's all very well, but we have advanced somewhat since ...

CARETAKER (*turns back to* WRIGHT): Won't do this school any harm havin' a few older members of staff. Respect, that's what's important — standards, discipline — honour — cleanliness. (*We hear the kids banging again*) There they go again, see. Another quarter of an hour, an' then ... (*He shivers*) I didn't go away, you know, oh no, not me ... (*Turns back, starts casually flicking through the records, interspersed with sudden scurries of words*) this was my holiday, stayin' here, bein' able t'walk the corridors without fear of standin' in the Phantom Crapper's mess, not havin' t'worry about bein' spat on from behind, pushed down the stairs, knocked t'the ground at the end of every lesson ... ah yes ... (*The records start slipping and falling onto the floor*)

MR WRIGHT: Surely things aren't that ...

CARETAKER: We'll see it all again before the day's out, smokin' in the toilets, sniffin' glue in woodwork, fightin', fartin', filth an' obscenities all over the walls ... (*As he builds himself up and the records fly about, we see* MISS McKENSIE *come down the corridor carrying the record*) ... bad manners, cheek, insolence, semolina spread across the canteen tables, long hair, bad teeth, pimples, black-heads ... (*Turns as* MISS McKENSIE *enters — he sees* MISS McKENSIE. *Approaches her, walking straight past* WRIGHT)

MR WRIGHT: It has been scientifically established that today's children are in fact ...

CARETAKER (*tries to grab the record*): Thank you, Miss ... just what I ... (*She shields it from him. She walks towards the chairs, he follows her. We hear the kids banging again. Louder*) No, you see, it's ... it's not what you ... (*He is close to her. Some menace. She backs away. He moves forward again.* MR WRIGHT *walks across*)

27

MR WRIGHT: Perhaps if you've lost something I can be ...
CARETAKER (*moving away rapidly towards the door*): No, no, nothing, nothing at all. I was just tidying up. (WRIGHT *looks at the mess of records*)
MISS McKENSIE: Mr Jackson. (*He hesitates, then turns around again. Pause*) It is ten to nine. You can let the children in now.

(*He goes to say something, stops, walks muttering out of the room, towards the emergency doors, stage right.* MISS McKENSIE *sits down with the record.* WRIGHT *approaches her. She, inevitably, nods.*)

MR WRIGHT: Ah good morning, how do you do? – Ronald Wright.

(*He holds out his hand. She nods again, he holds his hand out still, then takes it back.*)
(*The* CARETAKER *is opening the doors with a large bunch of keys. The noise outside increases. Then half a dozen lads between 14 and 16 pile out from behind the door. Couple of black lads, and most of the group in an attempt at a school uniform, but little pride.*)

FIRST BOY (*as the* CARETAKER *scuttles away with the keys*): 'You rang.' (*Laughter*)
SECOND BOY: Look at all them keys. It's like Frankenstein's castle.
FIRST BOY: It is Frankenstein's castle.
THIRD BOY: Every classroom a dungeon.
FIRST BOY: The gymnasium as the torture chamber. (*Laughs*) My old feller came up about Haddock last year, y'know. Gorra grip of him in the corridor.
SECOND BOY: Did he?
FIRST BOY: Yeah, told Haddock he wasn't hittin' me hard enough. (*Mirthless laugh*)
FOURTH BOY: My dad couldn't give a toss. Asked me Mam who our Kevin's friend was the other day – an' it was me. (*Mumbled agreements as two girls enter, go towards the corridor*) Hello girls, have a nice holiday, did y'? (*They ignore him*) Did y' miss us? We missed you.
FIRST GIRL: Aaahhh, his Action Man must have broke. (*They laugh*)

Act One

FIRST BOY: 'Ey, did y'hear about Jackie? She made page three ... in the Beano.
FIRST GIRL: Ah sod off! (*They go off*)
FOURTH BOY: Well, nothin's changed.
SECOND BOY: I wonder who we'll have this year.
FIRST BOY: Who cares. They're all the same.
THIRD BOY: Noddy's all right. (*They all nod at each other*)
FIRST BOY: Yeah.

(*They approach the staffroom door. It is open. The* FOURTH BOY *looks in. Friendly*)

FOURTH BOY: All right, Noddy? (*He waves*)
MISS McKENSIE (*without looking*): Hello Big Ears.

(THE BOYS *laugh, the* FOURTH BOY *pushes at a couple of them, they move towards the top of the corridor.*

FIRST BOY: Come on, let's go an' look f'some first years. (*Off*)
MISS McKENSIE: It won't be long now. (*She looks at the record.* WRIGHT *looks at his watch*)
MR WRIGHT (*eager to talk*): Soon.
MISS McKENSIE: They'll be marching in, taking over.
MR WRIGHT: I'm looking forward to it. I've waited so long.
MISS McKENSIE: The time has come. I always said it would. The writing's on the wall already.
MR WRIGHT: Spray cans. They are a nuisance, aren't they? I stopped selling them in my shop.
MISS McKENSIE: Just like before; the black shirts everywhere.
MR WRIGHT (*puzzled for the first time*): I'm not over-opposed to a certain lack of school uniform. Some of the new fashions are quite attractive.
MISS McKENSIE: Mosley and his mob.
MR WRIGHT: I don't know their names yet, of course, but I'll soon spot the troublemakers.
MISS McKENSIE: They're gaining strength every day.
MR WRIGHT: Growing boys ... it's inevitable. (*Pause*) I'm new here, as you've probably noticed. (*Laughs*) My name is Wright, Ronald Wright. I teach sociology.

29

MISS McKENSIE: It's all history now ...
MR WRIGHT: Erm ... no, not really, in fact not at all ...
MISS McKENSIE: ... But the same mistake's being made all over again. And this time, they're starting with the children. It can't go on. I must do something, but I would be wasting my time telling them. I tried again before, but nobody listens to me any more.
MR WRIGHT: Have you tried the new teaching methods?
MISS McKENSIE: The old looney with her lady lover. Ah, I know, I have seen the toilet walls.
MR WRIGHT (*pause*): Are you ... I mean, are we talking about the same thing? (*He looks at her. She is nodding*) Ah ...
MISS McKENSIE: No.
MR WRIGHT: Oh. I see. Well, by jove, that reminds me. (*He stands*) Just look at the time already. It's been very nice talking to you, I'm sure you'll get better soon. (*He goes towards the door*) You don't happen to know where the er men's ... mmmm, I expect I'll find it. (*He goes out*)
MISS McKENSIE: We always kept our beliefs very much to ourselves, yet our beliefs were always there, they never altered ... we shared the same values, Rose and I, we were very close, though ... though Daddy never liked her ... I remember ... we viewed the world through a closed window, but we saw the same things, and we suffered the same prejudices. We have learnt, people like Rose and I, what prejudice is all about ... she was stronger than I was ... am ... she would want me to make a stand, and I will make a stand ... we were very close though Daddy disapproved ... (*Louder*) ... the flame is going out ... soon all that will be left will be the smear of black smoke ... the smell of a burnt-out candle ...

(*As she slumps back into her seat, the lads return down the corridor. WRIGHT has closed the door of the staffroom behind him. A couple of them knock on the door as they go past and then move off quickly.*)

FOURTH BOY: We've only been in here five minutes an' I'm bored

Act One

already. (*They see the new boy arrive again, through the emergency doors*)
FIRST BOY: Hang on, hang on, what've we got here then? (*Slowly gather around him*)
THIRD BOY: I haven't seen one of these f'ages.
SECOND BOY: Not since this time last year.
NEW BOY: Excuse me ...
FIRST BOY: Manners an' all.
FOURTH BOY: He'll learn. (*They have surrounded him*)
FIRST BOY: Remember our first day?
THIRD BOY: The toilets?
FIRST BOY: School custom. Tradition as it were.
FOURTH BOY: A tour of the toilet bowls.
SECOND BOY: A close inspection.
FOURTH BOY: And a quick flush for good luck.
FIRST BOY: Happy days.
FOURTH BOY: Our turn now.
NEW BOY (*primly*): You touch me an' I'll tell the Headmaster.
FOURTH BOY: Ooooooh!
SECOND BOY: You mean you've seen him?
THIRD BOY: Lucky you, what's he look like?
FIRST BOY: Christopher Lee?

(MR WRIGHT *approaches from the corridor, looking for the toilets. Stops right by the gang. They just watch him.*)

MR WRIGHT: Good morning, boys. (*Pause. No reply. He hesitates, walks past, gets to far stage right, realises that he can go no further, apart from outside the school, returns*) I'm er new here, would you mind telling me where the staff ... toilets are, please?
FIRST BOY: Down the corridor, second turn on the right, through the double doors, along the third corridor on your left, second right, first left after the archway. Can't miss them. Sir.
MR WRIGHT: Thank you very much.
FIRST BOY (*as the others giggle*): S'nothin'.

(*He lets* MR WRIGHT *get a few feet away from him and then shouts in a high pitched voice: 'Looney'.* MR WRIGHT *turns.* THE BOYS

31

point to the NEW BOY *behind his back.* WRIGHT *hesitates, then turns back, goes off down the corridor.)*

FIRST BOY: We'll have him. See the state of him, looks like an interior decorator in a nut house. (*The others laugh*)

SECOND BOY (*snatching the* NEW BOY's *bag*): I wonder what's in here?

FOURTH BOY: Be the usual kind of first-year rubbish – rubbers, rulers, pencils ...

SECOND BOY (*holding it aloft*): PE kit!

FIRST BOY: Oh! Haddock will be pleased.

NEW BOY: *Leave it alone!*

FIRST BOY: That's no way t'talk t'your elders, boy.

SECOND BOY: Save it f'y'teachers.

NEW BOY: Give me back my kit – or I'll tell!

FIRST BOY: We're only tryin' t'help y' ...

FOURTH BOY: ... find the toilets.

FIRST BOY: Oh no, we wouldn't do a thing like that.

FOURTH BOY: Wouldn't we?

FIRST BOY: Course not. (*Takes the PE kit off the* SECOND BOY) Here you are, kidder, we were only jokin' with y'. (*Gives him the kit back*) Now, what d'y' want t'know?

NEW BOY (*still suspicious*): Where the Assembly Hall is.

FIRST BOY: No problem.

FOURTH BOY: It's just past the toilets.

FIRST BOY: Take no notice, you can trust me. We'll show you where it is. It's over here. (*Points stage left*) We have t'go up this corridor. Did they tell you *why* you have to bring your PE kit on your first day?

NEW BOY: No, it just said in the letter ...

FIRST BOY: So you haven't heard of the first-year combined kit inspection and assembly then?

FOURTH BOY: Eh? (*Glared at by* FIRST BOY) Oh. Oh aye.

NEW BOY (*softening*): I don't really like PE.

FOURTH BOY: Who does?

NEW BOY: No, you see, I get these dizzy spells.

FIRST BOY: Dizzy spells? That won't be good enough for

Haddock. Sudden death's the only excuse he accepts. Anyway, don't worry about that now. We'll get you ready for Assembly. (*They walk towards the corridor*) Another thing you should know about is that the first years always stand with the teachers on the first day. Did you know that? (*The* NEW BOY *shakes his head*) That's another custom we have here. There you are, y'see, stick with us an'y'won't go far wrong, we'll show you the ropes. Come on ... (*Couple of them snigger. They approach the end of the corridor.* DEAN *enters. The* FIRST BOY *tries to avoid him*)

MR DEAN: Logmond ... Logmond! (*He stops*) Here a minute.

FIRST BOY (*to the others*): I'll catch you up, all right? (*They go off. We see other pupils drift in and up the corridor*)

MR DEAN: Here — I won't bite you. (*The boy slowly approaches, refuses to look at* DEAN *throughout, and looks bored*)

FIRST BOY: Wha'?

MR DEAN: You know 'Wha''.

FIRST BOY: I forgot to come.

MR DEAN: I don't believe you.

FIRST BOY: Suit y'self. (*Turns away*)

MR DEAN: Look, a lad with your talent ... *Turn around!* (*He does so, but still looks away*) Who do you think you are — James Dean?

FIRST BOY: Who was he — your Dad?

MR DEAN: Look son ...

FIRST BOY: Don't call me son.

MR DEAN: Look Logmond, if you cause me any more trouble in class I'll have to ...

FIRST BOY: Yeah? Y'll have t'wha'?

MR DEAN (*pause*): I'll have to ask your parents to come up to school.

FIRST BOY (*laughs*): Oh aye yeah — they wouldn't come up here f'a big clock — never mind you.

MR DEAN (*pause, then quietly*): Go on, clear off.

(*The* FIRST BOY *smiles, turns away.* DEAN *watches him go, turns, head down, enters the staffroom.*

No More Sitting on the Old School Bench

We focus on the staffroom as DEAN enters. He goes across to his art folder and begins sorting it out. MISS McKENSIE faces front, still holding the record. HADDOCK enters, as he was before, apart from changing into training shoes. Stands downstage for some seconds, staring out. Picks up his timetable, looks at it, screws it up into a ball, kicks it. Enter MRS SWIFT and WRIGHT. She is already beginning to wilt.)

MR WRIGHT: ... above all else, I want you to understand, Freda, that my main concern lies not with myself, but with the quality of the lesson ...

MRS SWIFT *(as she goes towards her timetable)*: But the position is, I'm afraid, Mr ... *Ronald*, that the Headmaster always gives new members of staff Room 12.

MR WRIGHT: Yes, yes, but you see, I aim to set my standards high, and it will not help me to maintain those selfsame standards with the background of boilers, bouncing feet and electric saws.

MRS SWIFT: Indeed, indeed ... *(To everyone)* Hasn't Miss Kite arrived yet?

MR HADDOCK: You must be joking. She'll send a sick note to her own funeral, that one.

MR WRIGHT: There is just one thing ...

MRS SWIFT *(to WRIGHT)*: Look, I'll mention it to the Headmaster ... when he arrives. *(Again, generally)* Oh, she can't be ill again.

MR HADDOCK: Definitely a suitable case for redeployment, wouldn't you say, Mr Dean?

MR DEAN *(ignoring HADDOCK)*: Is she teaching, first lesson?

MRS SWIFT *(looking at the timetable)*: 5S.

MR DEAN: Oh bloody hell. *(Looks at his timetable)* Not already. Not first lesson.

MRS SWIFT: Are you free first? *(She looks at the timetable)*

MR HADDOCK: 'Are you free?'

MR DEAN: Yeah ...

MR WRIGHT: About Room 12 ... *(The bell goes)* What's that?

MR HADDOCK: It's a bell.

MR DEAN: Five minutes.
MR WRIGHT: Oh, I see. Freda ... (*A mad dash of kids race up the corridor past the staffroom; they all listen*) Freda ...
MRS SWIFT: You'll have to excuse me ... (*Turns away from* MR WRIGHT) Would you mind looking after 5S, Graham?
MR DEAN: No, it's all right.
MR HADDOCK: Course it's all right. He'll take his soap box with him. I mean, 5S, must be nearly old enough to join the Young Socialists. I can see it now – PE next lesson – all these little punks walking in the gym and refusin' t'get undressed and take their safety pins out, saying things like, 'Er, Karl Marx never did no PE, y'know, Sir, an' it didn't affect him, he saved mankind. Mr Dean told us.'
MR DEAN: What a joker you are, Haddock. And what a pity I have 5S second lesson as well as first now. (*Brandishes his timetable*) Isn't it about time you learnt to read a timetable, you're a big boy now.
MR HADDOCK: I don't think so.
MR DEAN: Look for yourself. (*Pushes his timetable at him. They both look*)
MR WRIGHT: I have a small suggestion to make, Freda ...
MRS SWIFT (*as* HADDOCK *then looks over her shoulder at the master timetable*): Yes, but please, not just ...
MR HADDOCK: We've both got them. (*He laughs*)
MRS SWIFT: Oh no!
MR DEAN: At the same time.
MR HADDOCK: That will be fun. Handstands and murals.
MR WRIGHT: Er, excuse me ...
MR DEAN: And I clash fourth lesson with Maisie. (*Points*) Look.
MRS SWIFT: Every year ... every ... bloody year. I ask him, I ask him to let me do the timetable, and every year he 'umms' and 'arrs' and disappears with it, and every year we have woodwork classes in the gym, biology in the tech. drawing room, one class for two teachers, two classes for one teacher ... I don't know ... (*The bell rings again*)
MR DEAN: Three minutes to registration.
MR HADDOCK: On your marks, get set ...

MRS SWIFT: Registration! And the registers are in the secretary's office.
MR DEAN: And she is in the boss's car.
MR HADDOCK: You never know, they might be in a multiple car-crash. No survivors. That's one way of getting rid of him.
MRS SWIFT: All right, all right ... (*Looks around*) Look, Graham, I'm supposed to be with the first years now in B block, could you do me a favour and go down and settle them for me? And on the way, ask the caretaker if any of his keys will open the boss's room?
MR DEAN: Okay. (*He walks towards the door*)

(*Some more kids go up the corridor towards the staffroom.*)

MR DEAN (*gets to the door, sees the kids running*): Hey, slow down. (*They do so. He follows after them*)
MR WRIGHT: If you could just spare me a few seconds, Freda ...
MRS SWIFT (*tonelessly*): Anything to help ...
MR WRIGHT: I don't want to make this into a big issue, but Room 12 ...
MRS SWIFT: Yes, go on, you want to have bomb-making demonstrations in there?
MR WRIGHT: No, I was just thinking, if it was a nice day, could I take the children out onto the field?
MR HADDOCK: Where the only diversions will be the girls' netball, the boys' football, the trees, the sky, the sun, passing aeroplanes and ...
MR WRIGHT: Mr Haddock, I was only ...
MR HADDOCK: Donald, if you don't mind. I do so dislike formality, don't you? (*He turns away from* WRIGHT)
MRS SWIFT (*slowly, as if to a child*): As soon as Assembly is over, I will have lots and lots of time to deal with your ... your ideas, but right now my only concern is trying to get this part of the school somewhere near normality. This is the first day of the first term, we have a lot of children who have never been here before. We are also lacking in certain basic requirements, such as a Headmaster, the secretary, a member of staff, the registers, a co-ordinated and happy staffroom ...

MR WRIGHT: So you don't think it's a good idea? (*Pause.* MRS SWIFT *giggles suddenly, uncontrollably. Walks away towards the chairs*)
MRS SWIFT: I think I'll have a baby.
MR WRIGHT: A ... baby?
MR HADDOCK: Really Freda, you should get a grip of yourself. You don't usually start saying that till at least half term.
MRS SWIFT (*sitting down*): No, seriously, you know ... it seems such an inviting prospect ... morning sickness, forty-two inch waist and nappies ... yes, a baby.
MR HADDOCK: I wouldn't bother if I were you. It's cruel bringing a child into the world these days. It's bound to have to go to school one day.
MRS SWIFT: Not all schools are like this one, Don. (*He looks at her*) And you know it. Some schools ... lots of schools are actually ... nice. They are. Considering the mess-ups and the fact that what passes for a comprehensive system in this country is still in its infancy, they really do work. When I go on courses and ... and I meet teachers who are ... happy ... fulfilled. Have headmasters that they can talk to instead of laugh at ... I just wonder what I'm doing here. Why I don't do something. Positive. Like leaving.
MR WRIGHT: I have another idea. Perhaps if I took them in the qu—
MR HADDOCK: Look, there's a good fellow, I'm sure you are really, I know it's all new to you, and you want to do your best, and you're probably standing here thinking what a bunch of awkward, strange, ignorant sods we are, and us *teachers* as well, and this a staffroom where honour and decency and belief should run unbridled, but just for two minutes or so, shut up, will you?
MR WRIGHT: I just ...
MR HADDOCK: *Please.*

(*Silence.* MRS SWIFT *stands, goes back to the timetable, starts writing amendments and billets-doux.* HADDOCK *turns away and lights a cigarette.* WRIGHT *looks at them for some time, then just stands there.*

We see more pupils drift in, side stage right. Through the auditorium comes JACKSON. *He sees a group of lads — selects only the black lads — then asks one white boy to wait behind.* JACKSON *forces the black lads to carry six portable chairs. Bullies and chivvies them into placing them into position in the assembly area. One or two place them the wrong way around till he tells them off. He lets them go. As they drift off, we see two more boys enter with a shopping bag each. They look highly suspicious, but* JACKSON *is approaching the boy whom he has asked to stay behind. The two likely lads take six cushions out of their bags, place them on the chairs, look furtively around, laugh, then run off. The* CARETAKER *is walking with the white boy towards the corridor.*)

CARETAKER: Saw your dad last night ... at our little ... meeting. Said you shared the same ... views. You know. Felt the same about the same things.

WHITE BOY: Yeah, I wanted t'come but ...

CARETAKER: Well, perhaps not just yet. But soon. Very soon. You can be of some considerable help, however ... Jimmy, isn't it? (*The boy nods*) You see ... we're organising a few of the brighter boys in the school, building up a dossier on the troublemakers, planning a kind of ... magazine to help those of you who are on our side, and those of you who are on our side but don't know it yet.

(DEAN *comes down the corridor.* JACKSON *moves away from the boy.*)

MR DEAN: Mr Jackson ...

CARETAKER: Very good, Jimmy, well done. Young Edwards here, Mr Dean, put out all the staff chairs for Assembly, all on his ...

MR DEAN: You must have found his vocation in life, Mr Jackson, because it certainly isn't Art, is it, Jimmy?

WHITE BOY: No, Sir.

MR DEAN: Perhaps you can draw a chair in the next lesson. (*Turns to the* CARETAKER *as the* BOY *drifts off*) Have you got any keys to the Headmaster's office, Mr Jackson?

CARETAKER (*sweetness and light, taking his keys out*): I don't think so, Mr Dean, but it'll be no trouble at all to check my box of spares. (*Looks at the* BOY *as he goes*) I'll er speak to you about that matter again, Edwards. (*Turns back to* DEAN) Keen fisherman, you see. Wanted my advice. (*Smiles at* DEAN) I know his father. Yes well, right, the key ... (*Goes quickly up the corridor.* DEAN *looks puzzled, stares at both the* CARETAKER *and the* BOY, *then enters the staffroom*)

MR DEAN: The first years are as quiet as mice, the caretaker's been nice to me, and you'll never guess who I've seen.

MR HADDOCK: Shirley Williams come to give us a pep-talk? 'Now, look here you lot, you bloody miserable rabble, this just isn't ...'

MR DEAN: Miss Kite.

MR HADDOCK & MRS SWIFT: *Miss Kite?*

MR HADDOCK: In a passing ambulance?

MR DEAN: Walking down the school drive. All the kids asking her if she was a new teacher.

MR HADDOCK: Ah, poor girl, really must be ill now. No other explanation.

MRS SWIFT: One problem solved anyway. (*The registration bell goes*)

MR HADDOCK: Seconds out, first round ...

(*We see the* HEADMASTER *approaching.*)

MRS SWIFT: All we need now is ... (*The* HEADMASTER *bustles through the doorway*)

MR GRANT: Well, well well, good timing, yes what, right on the bell. Welcome back everyone, sorry about the delay, petrol pump trouble, everything sorted out now, been holding the fort, Freda, good good good. (*As he speaks, he walks over to the wall, adjusts the Queen's painting, glances at the notice board, goes over to the small curtained window, pulls the curtains until they are the same width. He will never look anyone in the face for more than the briefest glance. Returns toward the table piled with books*) Yes oh yes, here we are, back again. (*Claps his hands together*) Well, mustn't keep you, must we, on with the job, hey? (*Pause*) Registration, yes?

MRS SWIFT: The registers, Mr Grant.

MR GRANT: Oh yes, of course, Mrs Andrews will be along in a moment, I seem to have mislaid my keys. (*He begins to fiddle with one of the books*) Er ... everyone had a good holiday? Freda? France again, yes? (*She nods*) That's the stuff. Good weather?

MRS SWIFT (*nods again*): Yes, but one or two problems about the ... (*She goes to indicate the timetable*)

MR GRANT (*holds up his hands*): You don't have to tell me. I know what it was. Accommodation, wasn't it? Am I right? Always the same, the French, been invaded too many times, no respect for their guests, oh yes, that's what it is, I prefer Spain myself.

MRS SWIFT (*holding the timetable up, to no effect*): Yes, but it's a question of ...

MR GRANT: Politics? Really Freda? I had no idea. Yes, well, never mind, Franco's dead now. Talking about politics, what about you, Mr Dean? Have a good holiday?

MR DEAN: Yes thank you, but I wouldn't have had if I'd ... (*Picks up the* Guardian)

MR GRANT: Russia? Yugoslavia? The beaches of East Germany? (*He laughs*)

MR DEAN: North Wales, actually. However, this morning ...

MR GRANT: Yes, pretty revolting lot, the Welsh, aren't they? (*He laughs. Alone. Pulls at the book he is fidgeting with. They all start cascading onto the floor*) Ooops!

(*Pause. Nobody wants to help him pick them up. HADDOCK and DEAN look at each other. WRIGHT comes forward, puts his wallpaper down, begins to help the HEADMASTER. MRS SWIFT puts her timetable against the table. She starts to pick some books up in a resigned manner. WRIGHT and GRANT meet each other on the floor under the table. WRIGHT offers his hand. At first he is not recognised by GRANT, who looks over to MRS SWIFT.*)

MR GRANT: Erm, yes, er ...

MRS SWIFT: Mr Wright, the new member of the staff whom you appointed, if you ...

MR WRIGHT: There is something I ...

MR GRANT: Ah yes, what! Fine, good, excellent, enjoying it?

Act One

(*Shakes hands – still on their knees*) I trust you've met Mrs Swift? Mrs Swift.

MRS SWIFT: We have met.

MR GRANT: No problems, so far?

MR WRIGHT: Please don't misunderstand me, but Roo—

MR GRANT (*standing up and moving away*): Of course, bound to be teething troubles, but not to worry, we all muddle through, don't we, yes, that's the spirit. Oh yes, well ... (*Looks around*) Mmmmm. (*Looks at his watch. We also hear* MISS McKENSIE *start to murmur to herself*)

MR DEAN (*quickly getting in*): About this redeployment issue, Headmaster, I would like to see you sometime today if ...

MR GRANT: Today, oh, today, well ...

MR DEAN: Before any action is organised. (MISS McKENSIE *gets louder*)

MR GRANT: Action? Organised? Oh yes, well, let's not be too hasty, shall we? Pardon, Miss McKensie, yes ... (*Turns back*) I realise that there er must be a certain amount of emotion on the subject, but I for one am not in any state of panic. Yes, I have every faith that er something will ... that we can all work this one out ... that it will all blow over without us having to take any action at all. Yes.

MR DEAN: So I can report back to the union meeting tonight that you plan to do nothing?

MR GRANT: Ye— ... I never said that! Did I say that, Freda? Now now, young man, I had enough of this last year, don't put words into my mouth ...

MISS McKENSIE: Someone has to ... (*They all turn around*)

MR GRANT: I beg your ...

MISS McKENSIE: Someone has to do something ... we can't wait any longer.

MR GRANT: The registers will be here as soon as Mrs Andrews finds the caretaker. Quite regrettable, I realise ... (*He starts to play with the arm of the broken duplicator*) My fault entirely. To tell you the truth, I had a slight accident with my cornflakes at breakfast, and in the rush to get here, I ... (*The arm comes off in his hand, he looks at it, mesmerized*) I ch— ... (*Tries to put it back on*) ... I left my school keys in ... it seems to be broken ... in my pocket ... yes, well ... (*Puts the arm on top of the duplicator*) When I changed my trousers, I ... right.

(*The* CARETAKER *comes to the door.*)

CARETAKER: Mr Grant ...
MR GRANT: Ah, the very man ...
CARETAKER: It's Miss Kite, Mr Grant.
MR GRANT: Yes, I saw her too, quite remarkable, but about the registers, have you seen the secretary?
CARETAKER: No, it's like this, she's had a bad accident.
MR GRANT: Mrs Andrews?
CARETAKER: Miss Kite. She got to the door an' a massive big Alsatian pulled her to the ground. It was terrible, the blood ...
MR GRANT: Er, well, the first aid room ...
CARETAKER: I give you the keys for that last term, when you fell off the stage in Assembly ...
MR GRANT: Quite, quite. So you haven't got the key to my office either?
CARETAKER: No sir, remember, you dropped them all down that grid and ...
MR GRANT: Indeed, *thank you*, Mr Jackson ... now this is quite tricky ...
CARETAKER: And some of the upper school are runnin' wild, Headmaster. They keep ...
MRS SWIFT: Right, I'll go down and see Miss Kite. Where is she, Mr Jackson?
CARETAKER: On the step outside, Mrs ...
MRS SWIFT: The rest of you go to your registration classrooms, count heads, take names if necessary, but let's show our faces for goodness sake.
MR GRANT: Yes!
MRS SWIFT: And you, Headmaster, would you go down to B block and see the first years into Assembly. And as soon as you can, everybody, let's have the school in the Hall, it's well past nine o'clock now.

Act One

(HADDOCK, DEAN, WRIGHT *move towards the door.* MRS SWIFT *goes across to* MISS McKENSIE.

MR GRANT: I er seem to have mislaid my notes for Assembly, Freda, you couldn't by any chance ... take it for me?
MRS SWIFT: There's no guarantee that I'll be there, Headmaster. If Miss Kite is badly injured, I'll have to ring for an ambulance and ...
MR GRANT: Yes, well, I expect I'll find something to say.
MRS SWIFT: I'm sure you will. (*He stands there*) The first years ...
MR GRANT: Ah, yes, B. Block. The Assembly Hall.
MRS SWIFT: And as soon as you can spare me a minute, I'd like to spend some time with you on the timetable.
MR GRANT (*goes quickly*): Of course, yes, I think I might just slip home after Assembly, get my keys, you know ... yes ... (*Off. The* CARETAKER *is still in the room. Loitering*)
MRS SWIFT (*by* MISS McKENSIE, *quietly*): Maisie. Maisie. (*She looks at* MRS SWIFT) What kind of a dog did you get, Maisie?
MISS McKENSIE: A big dog. (*Looks at* MRS SWIFT) An Alsatian. But nobody will look after ...
MRS SWIFT: Oh Maisie. It'll have to go.
MISS McKENSIE: I had hoped it would bite someone else.
MRS SWIFT (*pause*): Let's have a chat at lunchtime, shall we? Sort ourselves out. (*No answer. She turns away*) Where is the dog now, Mr Jackson?
CARETAKER: It went towards the Infants.
MRS SWIFT: That's all we need. Use my phone would you, and warn Miss Watson. (*She goes out*)

(JACKSON *goes towards the door, turns and looks at* MISS McKENSIE. *He walks across slowly towards her. She notices him, hugs the record to her chest.*)

CARETAKER: Give it to me ... come on, give it to me. (*For the first time he seems a frightening figure*) All you have to do is give it to me. (*Stands in front of her*) I won't tell anyone. (*She stands up. He gets closer. She moves to one side*) I won't hurt you. (*He moves after her*) Just give it to me, an' it'll all be forgotten. There now. (*She *backs aways towards the table with the books on it. She gets one side, he the other. He tries to grab the record, knocks some books over, races around the other side. They tussle. He pushes her)* I said give it to me! (*Grabs hold of her, wrenches the record from her grasp, knocks her to the floor by the books. Turns away in triumph as the* HEADMASTER *comes down the corridor in his usual flap. Both approach the door*)

MR GRANT: Yes, Assembly, yes ... (*Sees the* CARETAKER *with the record*) That's it, I'll play them some music. (*Takes the record off the* CARETAKER) Hymns, just the job, thank you, Mr ... (*Sees* MISS McKENSIE *on the floor*)

CARETAKER: No, you can't ...

MR GRANT: Had a fall, Miss McKensie? Silly place to put books, I'm sure. (*Goes across to her, lifts her up*) No bones broken, I hope? What a morning.

MISS McKENSIE: That record, he ...

CARETAKER: I never!

MR GRANT: Yes, so fortunate. I was going to read from the Gospels otherwise. Mr Jackson, would you be so good as to carry the record player into the Assembly Hall for me? (*He walks over to it*)

CARETAKER: It's broken!

MR GRANT: Are you certain? (*Switches it on*) Seems fine to me. (*Looks at the LP cover*) Now then. Yes, oh yes, 'Morning Has Broken'. But not the record player. (*Points*) There you are, off you go.

(JACKSON *lifts the player up, hits the side with his fist, looks as though he will get around the corner and throw it against the nearest wall. The* HEADMASTER *is close behind him, however. They go out together.*)

MR GRANT: Miss McKensie, hurry now, first Assembly of the term, make an impression ...

MISS McKENSIE (*as she goes slowly out*): I'll put the record on for you, Headmaster.

(*The lights dim on the staffroom.*

Act One

Front stage. We see four lines of pupils moving into position in front of the chairs which represent the stage of the Assembly Hall. Two rows of boys, two rows of girls, smallest at the front representing the first years. The boys at the back are soon bored and fidgeting, whispering, chewing, nudging each other.

HADDOCK *and* DEAN *come on stage – standing at opposite ends to each other, occasionally pointing and threatening someone into line.* WRIGHT *appears with a list of names. He goes to sit in the centre.* DEAN *whispers to him; he moves to one side. The* CARETAKER *appears with the record player, puts it down heavily by* DEAN, *takes the lead off–stage.* MISS McKENSIE *watches him as she arrives. She goes after him. We see her yank at the lead; it comes back to her. The* CARETAKER *appears briefly, angrily, looks out, sees everyone looking at him, shoots back off stage.* MISS McKENSIE *finds a socket. The* HEADMASTER *walks on stage in his cape. The kids hum 'BATMAN'. He stands waiting for silence. He waits for some time, coughs, nothing happens.* HADDOCK *looks out.)*

MR HADDOCK: You – shut it. (*Silence.* HADDOCK *looks at* DEAN, *who makes sucking motions*)

MR GRANT: Yes, good morning, school. (*A few whispered attempts*) I said 'Good morning'. (*Bellows of 'Good morning' – some well over the top. But the* HEADMASTER *seems pleased*) That's better. (MRS SWIFT *appears stage left, walks across to stand by the* HEADMASTER. *He glances at her, whispers; she shakes her head*) So, another fresh start, another term starting here at Greenfields, new faces, young and old, a new beginning for us all. (*Pause*) I hope you all had a very enjoyable holiday, but above all, I hope and expect that you are returning this morning fresh and determined to make a ... a, to have a splendid term. Those of us who have always given our whole for others ... (*Some giggles*) quiet now, those who ... they will be rewarded, but those of you who have let the team down at times, let me say to you now, we start again today, the board is wiped clean, it is still not too late to come and join us. (*We hear some boys start to hum* 'Come and join us, come and join us.') Quiet, quiet, I won't have behaviour like ...

(*The* NEW BOY *is seen looking out from side stage. He walks nervously on stage in his gym kit. Laughter. He is standing by* MISS McKENSIE *and* MR DEAN. *The* HEADMASTER *twirls around, looks at him, double takes, hesitates, decides to ignore him.* MR DEAN *leans across to him. The* BOY *is upset.*)

MR GRANT: Yes, well, unfortunate . . . (*Looks again*) . . . stay there, boy, I'll deal with you in a moment. So now, I said be quiet, so now, in the spirit of a fresh start, I intend playing a very significant piece of music to you this morning. Listen to the words, and remember, we are on the threshold of a new beginning. Miss McKensie, would you be so kind.

(MISS McKENSIE *puts the needle on the record. The* HEADMASTER *looks all around him, indicates to the staff that they may sit. He sits down himself, fractionally in front of everyone else. His whooper cushion makes a loud farting noise. All the others do in turn, finishing with* MISS McKENSIE's. *The* HEADMASTER *jumps up, as do the rest of the staff.*)

MR GRANT: What the . . .!

(*A recording of a Hitler speech blares out. The staff turn and look at the record player, then at* MISS McKENSIE. *She smiles. The needle sticks on 'Sieg Heil'.*
  Lights out.
  We still hear the record till the house lights come on.)

ACT TWO

(*Staffroom. Just before break on the last day of the first half term.*)
(*The staffroom is much the same as it was before, expect that the pigeon holes are full of such stuff as stale sandwiches, gym shoes, track suit bottoms, raffle tickets, fold-up umbrellas, books. And the notice board is overwhelmed with notices. The duplicator is still broken. A different pile of books is on the duplicator table. We see the* TEA LADY *with her trolley coming into the staffroom. Teapot, cups, saucers. She moves the trolley in front of the record player.* HADDOCK *appears at the side of the auditorium, stage right. Gym shoes and normal dress, whistle around his neck, rolled up paper in one hand, basketball in the other.*)

MR HADDOCK (*shouting back*): Sefton! Sefton – get back in the changing room, you useless nicotine-stained knock-kneed lump. When the bell goes you can come out, and not until. (*Turns away, walks into the staffroom*)
TEA LADY: Good mornin', Mr Haddock. (*He walks past her, only turns as he nears the chairs*)
MR HADDOCK: What? Sorry ... oh yes, good morning. (*He sits down. Stares out*)

(*The* CARETAKER *comes down the corridor at a pace. Enters the staffroom holding a mop and a bucket.*)

CARETAKER (*to the* TEA LADY): Have you seen the Headmaster?
TEA LADY: No, Mr ...
CARETAKER: Look at this – just look at it! (*Holds his mop and*

bucket up. They are stuck together) Stuck together! A whole tube of that flamin' instant glue. The price of it an' all – nearly a pound a tube. A pound! An' the bloody stuiff's everywhere – the curtains in the hall glued together, the piano lid an' the dustbins ... I leave my shoes outside my office for two minutes, an' what happens – that's right, yes, glued t'tha flamin' floor! An' if I lay my hands on the joker who stuck my bike t'the ceilin' in A block ...

MR HADDOCK: Never mind, Mr Jackson, half-day strike today, courtesy of Mr Dean and his merry bunch of militants, and then a whole week's half term.

(*He rises as he talks, goes slowly over towards the teapot. The* TEA LADY *puts her hand on the teapot handle. The* CARETAKER *tugs at his mop and bucket. We hear noises off from the changing rooms.* HADDOCK *turns away towards the staffroom door, marches down the corridor towards the auditorium. The* CARETAKER *comes across to the* TEA LADY *as* HADDOCK *shouts.*)

MR HADDOCK: Sefton – are you deaf or daft, lad? What did I just say to you – now the lot of you, get in there ...

TEA LADY: Terrible, isn't it 'ey? (*Indicates his mop and bucket as the* CARETAKER *reaches over to pour a cup of tea. He stops*)

CARETAKER: What! I'll say so. The world's gone mad, it has, Mrs Murray. Mad. I ask you, where're they gettin' that kind of money, 'ey – a pound a tube. They've got more than you an' me, some of them. Used t'get a school bus once upon a time – now half of them get driven here by Securicor. (*Goes to take hold of the teapot again. He stops as the* TEA LADY *speaks*)

TEA LADY: Not like it used t'be, is it?

CARETAKER: Not like it used t'be, indeed. The good old days, 'ey? Remember? When this was a grammar school. A grammar school, with uniforms an' short hair ... an' Latin ... an' milk monitors. (*Again takes hold of the teapot, again releases it*) An' we're goin' t'be one again, mark my words, there'll be changes made. *Changes*, Mrs Murray.

TEA LADY: Er, yes. Changes.

Act Two

CARETAKER: It's time we all stood up t'be counted, d'you know that? The likes of us. You an' me. Don't you think?

TEA LADY: Oh er ... yes.

CARETAKER: Dead right you do. We all do, but what can we do on our own? Nothing, nothing at all. But together, those of us with similar views, united, now that's a different kettle of fish. (*Again, goes to pick up the teapot, stops, looks at her*) I hold meetin's, Mrs Murray, meetin's for people of like minds, people who've had it up to here of seein' this country goin' t'the dogs. And unless I'm very much mistaken ... Josie, you're one of those people. Aren't you?

TEA LADY: Well, you know, it's ... it's not like it used to be.

CARETAKER: And you know why – the politicians've gone soft: What we all want is a return of law an' order, back to the days of decency an' white faces. ... And y'know what my answers've been for years – bring back the birch an' the eleven plus, oh yes. By definition, if you passed the eleven plus, you were someone special, you were different, you were looked up to, you were hard workin', you were out for success, destined for a position of prestige ... (*Once more he has his hand on the handle of the teapot*) ... I can remember it well. (*Pause. He has a vision*)

TEA LADY: Did you pass the eleven plus then, Mr Jackson?

CARETAKER: Eh?

TEA LADY: Did you pass the eleven plus?

CARETAKER: Oh yes, of course, but my mother wanted me t'be a priest. Oh yes, I could have been someone, I could. I could, you know. However, the day will come all right ... (*He goes, finally, to lift up the teapot, pulls and tugs, till he realises that it is stuck to the trolley. He attempts to force it up, rattles the cups, the* TEA LADY *holding onto the trolley. He pushes it angrily away*) But what I would really like is an epidemic that wipes out everyone under the age of seventeen, an' prevents any more births 'til I'm past the age of ... retirement. That's my dream, that is. (*He takes up his mop and bucket, storms out towards the changing rooms. The* TEA LADY *looks confused*)

(*As soon as the* CARETAKER *leaves, we see the* HEADMASTER *and* MRS SWIFT *coming down the corridor.* MRS SWIFT *seems considerably more tired than before.*)

MR GRANT (*as they walk*): I well, yes, I know, Freda, but ...
MRS SWIFT: It was only two days ago that you sent a memo around all the staff in both schools saying that until this glue outbreak stopped, on no account was anyone to leave a class unattended, and now here you are, dragging me out of ...
MR GRANT: But this is urgent, it really ...
MRS SWIFT: You know what happened in the Biology lab last week – two frogs, a bull's eye and a skinned rat stuck together. On the skeleton's shoulder ...
MR GRANT: Indeed, but you see, I needed a word with you in private ... (*He looks into the staffroom – pokes his head around the door. He and the* TEA LADY *look at each other*) Er, hello ... (*Closes the door quickly*) Now then, well ...
MRS SWIFT: Yes?
MR GRANT: We can't go in there, I'm afraid. The tea ...
MRS SWIFT: Your room?
MR GRANT: I well ... it's temporarily ...
MRS SWIFT: You've mislaid your keys?
MR GRANT: Only momentarily. I'm sure they'll ...
MRS SWIFT: My room then ...
MR GRANT: Actually, no, unfortunately, there's a parent in there at the moment. She's rather upset, you see, and I thought it perhaps better if you saw her, woman to woman as it were. It's the mother of that dreadful boy who was on stage in his PE kit at the start of term ...
MRS SWIFT: Again? Good God, she's here more often than some of the kids, but at least she comes, which is more than you can say for most of the others. Bullying again, is it? (*She opens the staffroom door*)
MR GRANT: I didn't really ... you know how distasteful I find it having to talk to ... (*He blindly follows her in, realises he doesn't want to be there*) Erm, no, I'd rather speak to you in ...

Act Two

(*As they come in, the* TEA LADY *attempts to ladle some tea out of the pot with a cup. The steam burns and defeats her.* MRS SWIFT *approaches with the* HEADMASTER *in tow.*)

MRS SWIFT: It'll never replace using the spout, Mrs Murray.
TEA LADY: It's ... someone's stuck it to the trolley, an' I can't budge it.
MR GRANT (*in full posture*): Disgraceful, disgraceful. I expect immediate action on that one, Mrs Swift.
TEA LADY: I only left it for a minute an' well ...

(*The* HEADMASTER *proceeds to fidget around the room, altering the curtains, touching up the Queen's portrait, looking in the pigeon holes.*)

MRS SWIFT (*to the* TEA LADY): If I were you, I'd go down to the kitchens get another teapot, make another pot of tea. (*Moves her towards the doorway*) and upon your return, you will be greeted as a saviour. (*The* TEA LADY *goes out*. MRS SWIFT *turns and approaches the* HEADMASTER) What's the problem then?
MR GRANT: I've just told you, I didn't ask the woman ... oh, I see, yes, the er *problem*. (*Looks all around him*) It's ... (*Speaks quickly*) It's redeployment. I'm afraid I've rather let the matter shall we say ... (*Looks at her, looks away*) ... slide, in the hope, of course, that there would be another way out ... however, I have to give the two names into the Office today, and with this idiotic strike of Mr Dean's ...
MRS SWIFT: Today? This early?
MR GRANT: The understaffed schools have to know, so that they can select who they ...
MRS SWIFT: It's wonderful, isn't it? Can you imagine the first morning for the redeployed teachers in their new school – walking into the staffroom with 'reject' written all over them. Madness ...
MR GRANT: Nevertheless ...
MRS SWIFT: 'We must do our duty.' Who are you considering?
MR GRANT: Well, I er think it goes without saying that everyone

51

in the Main Block is erm unexpendable. I was rather looking towards ... (*Waves his hands about*) ... er, Miss Kite.

MRS SWIFT: The Invisible Woman. Whoever gets her will be well pleased. Who else?

MR GRANT (*not looking at her except for the briefest second*): And ... but ... I'm not absolutely su— ... I could be dissuaded about ... it's possibly rather personal ... not that I'm a vindictive man ... Mr Dean. (*He turns away*)

MRS SWIFT (*calmly*): Perhaps the best member of staff we have.

MR GRANT (*walking away*): Ever since he arrived he's been nothing but a thorn in my side, one union matter after another ... complaints, queries, ultimatums ... I mean, who does he think ... the *best* member of staff?

MRS SWIFT: Probably. If your criteria is the classroom. And I think that it should be, don't you?

MR GRANT: Mmmm, I'm not particularly *au fait* with that side of him. I rather leave that department in your capable hands, Freda.

MRS SWIFT: Yes. (*Pause*)

MR GRANT (*moving away again*): It just struck me that the general tone ... the administration of the school would be enhanced by his absence. I would, of course, give him the highest recommendation, an absolutely glowing reference, you know, highlighting his er undoubted skills ... his qualities ... his classroom activities ... (*He turns back hopefully to her but she remains impassive*)

MRS SWIFT: Always a good way of getting rid of someone.

MR GRANT: Yes, well, let's leave Mr Dean. For the moment. Er, who ... erm, did you have anybody in mind?

MRS SWIFT: Nobody. I leave that side of the school to you, Headmaster.

MR GRANT (*circling around her*): But if I was to, say, ask your opinion, just as a matter of interest, who would you say we could most do without?

(*She looks at him. We must be aware that he is the person she and the school could most do without.*)

Act Two

MRS SWIFT (*sighs*): Can we redeploy the caretaker?
MR GRANT: No, it has to be a member of staff. (*Pause*) Ah, I see, a joke. (*He laughs*) Incidentally, has all that business blown over, you know, the . . . remember, I delegated you to . . . the 'Hitler' episode . . .
MRS SWIFT: Miss McKensie ultimately had no proof. We did elicit from the caretaker that he'd started to hold meetings in the staffroom after hours, but he persisted in his story that it was a newly formed History Society. I pointed out to him that he needed permission to hold such meetings in school . . .
MR GRANT: Indeed, indeed . . .
MRS SWIFT: And he informed me that he had your consent.
MR GRANT: Oh. Oh yes, come to think of it . . .
MRS SWIFT: And when I asked him if I could join, he announced it was over-subscribed.
MR GRANT: Ah, what a pity. Still, good, good, I thought there would be a satisfactory explanation. (MRS SWIFT *looks at him, amazed*) Now, mmmm, Miss McKensie. What do you think? A possibility, heh?
MRS SWIFT (*trying hard to control herself*): I would be very reluctant for two reasons, Headmaster. Firstly, her examination results are the best in the Authority, year in, year out, and that's not something you can say about other members of staff . . .
MR GRANT: Of course, the examinations . . .
MRS SWIFT: And secondly, she is such an unusual . . . she is an eccentric, perhaps in some ways disturbed, certainly since the . . . her bereavement. She needs as much stability as possible. A change of school would be to her disadvantage, would not benefit whatever school she went to, and would do our pupils, who are used to her, a disservice. There is no way we could replace her.
MR GRANT: I thought as much. Yes. Out of the question. *Oh, I don't know, if only someone would volunteer!* It would make my job so much easier.
MRS SWIFT: I think perhaps I had better go and see Mrs Urquhart.
MR GRANT: Who? Mrs Urquhart? Do we have a . . .
MRS SWIFT: The boy's mother – in my room.

MR GRANT: Not to worry, I asked my secretary to make her a cup of tea. Let's just think for a moment. I don't want to make an important decision like this one without consulting you fully, Freda.

MRS SWIFT: I thought you wouldn't.

MR GRANT: Though I must say my mind was rather made up about Mr Dean ... (*He again looks in hope, but there is no joy*) Never mind, let me see ... (*Rubs his hands together*) Oh, come on ...

MRS SWIFT: I also have a class, and the bell is ... (*She goes towards the door*)

MR GRANT (*looks at his watch*): Yes, but you'll never get back there in time now.

MRS SWIFT: Look, do you really want my opinion?

MR GRANT: Oh, absolutely.

MRS SWIFT: The one member of staff we could justifiably lose for the complete benefit of the school is Mr Wright.

MR GRANT: Oh no no no. I don't think so, Not Mr Wright ... I have the greatest confidence in Mr Wright. I'm surprised at you, Freda ...

MRS SWIFT: Have you been past his classroom lately?

MR GRANT: It is not my policy to spy on my members of staff.

MRS SWIFT: No one's asking you to spy, Headmaster. Just spend some time down here, walk around the school occasionally. However much I may agree with his theories, in practice ... The noise from Mr Wright's classes has to be heard to be believed.

MR GRANT: Noise is no indication of failure, Freda. Silence is not golden to this generation, and I for one rejoice in it. Often noise is a sign of unbridled enthusiasm, a hubbub of activity, a passion for learning ...

MRS SWIFT: And in Mr Wright's case, a riot situation. Can I remind you of what happened last week ...

MR GRANT: I er don't need ...

MRS SWIFT: No other teacher I know would allow his class – his *sociology* class, mind – to take him on a cross-country run through Chinsley Woods, and then let them run away from him.

MR GRANT: A bit of tomfoolery. High spirits ...

MRS SWIFT: He was found at nine o'clock that night by the wardens in the Safari Park. Up a tree.

MR GRANT: I still feel that he has a lot to offer. It takes time to settle. We must give him an opportunity to learn through experience. And you must remember that I personally appointed him, you know. Mmmm, yes. (*Pause*) And not without some opposition from the Governors if I remember rightly.

MRS SWIFT: Ah, I understand now.

MR GRANT: A man must have a fair trial.

MRS SWIFT: It's just unfortunate that we have to serve the sentence with him.

MR GRANT: Time will tell, Freda. Time will tell. (*The bell goes*) I'm rarely wrong in my estimation of people. Mr Wright is going to be an asset to this school. He has qualities, hope and enthusiasm, a belief in the future, that reminds me very much of ... (*He preens*) ... well, you know ... like hearts. (*He laughs. We see a gang of lads with PE kit run up the corridor. Shouts and laughter.* GRANT *starts for the door as* MR HADDOCK *walks up the corridor towards the staffroom*) I'll keep you informed.

MRS SWIFT: There is one other matter, a personal matter, Headmaster, but affecting the school: I would like a few words with you before the end of the morning.

MR GRANT: Surely ... (HADDOCK *enters.* GRANT *stops, looks at him*) Ah, good morning, Mr Haddock. How are we today?

MR HADDOCK (*glances at* MRS SWIFT): Fine, just fine. (*Goes to walk away.* MR GRANT *follows him*)

MR GRANT: The family?

MR HADDOCK: Er ... the family?

MR GRANT: Keeping well?

MR HADDOCK: I was divorced four years ago, Headmaster.

MR GRANT (*quickly*): But they're keeping fine?

MR HADDOCK: I had no children.

MR GRANT: Ah, of course. Somewhat of a free agent then, as it were?

MR HADDOCK: You could say that.

MR GRANT: Free to come and go, no ties, no one to worry about if you decided to move around ... move on ... advance ...

MR HADDOCK (*looking again at* MRS SWIFT): You could say that as well. And you could also tell me what we're talking about.

MR GRANT: Ever forthright, Mr Haddock. Yes ... well, never mind, just an idea, nothing to worry about. Just yet. (*Turns away, then back again*) How long is it that you've been with us?

MR HADDOCK: Eleven years.

MR GRANT: That long? Eleven years. *Eleven* years. Never felt the need for a change, heh! Fresher pastures, such like, greener grass perhaps, who knows?

MR HADDOCK: I don't like grass. I get hay fever. (*Turns away.* MR GRANT *goes to follow him*)

MR GRANT: There's no need to be facetious, Mr ...

(*We hear an absolute tumult of shouting and laughter from side stage right. Getting nearer. We also hear the kids singing.*)

KIDS: Glue, glue,
    Glorious glue,
    Nothing quite like it
    For sticking to you ...

(*We see* MR WRIGHT *totally surrounded by a large number of pupils. He approaches the staffroom as* MRS SWIFT *and* MR GRANT *go to the door.*)

MR GRANT: Quiet now, come on, quiet ... (*Little reaction from the kids, but when they see* MRS SWIFT, *they quieten down, one by one*)

MRS SWIFT: Out, go on, out into the playground.

(*The kids drift off in dribs and drabs. Some sniggering as they depart. We see that* MR WRIGHT *has a chair stuck solidly to the seat of his trousers. He is embarrassed but desperately cheerful. Enters the staffroom as* MRS SWIFT *stares at him in disbelief. She turns to he* HEADMASTER, *who refuses to look at her.*)

Act Two

MR GRANT: Yes well . . . erm, must be getting back. I'm expected, you know, if you could look after . . . (*Points in* MR WRIGHT's *direction*) . . . I tell you what, I'll see to that parent for you — yes? Good. (*Walks slightly away*) I'll erm be over at dinner hour . . . (*He sees* MR DEAN *enter the corridor, carrying a number of placards with him, signs such as 'More teachers, not less', 'Redeploy the redeployers', 'No to redeployment',* GRANT *tries to read the posters as* MR DEAN *goes past. Says nothing, but grimaces*) . . . let you know what I've . . . my decision about the . . . you know. (*Scuttles off up the corridor.* MRS SWIFT *enters the staffroom*)

(MR DEAN *has put his signs down in a corner, is looking at* MR WRIGHT *who wanders briefly about, then notices the others looking at him. He promptly sits down on his chair. Smiles.* MRS SWIFT *approaches him.*

Outside in the corridor, we see the FIRST, SECOND *and* FOURTH BOYS *swagger slowly downstage just as the* NEW BOY *comes from side right of the auditorium. As soon as he sees the older boys, he freezes. They approach, stand around him, don't do anything, just stand there above him in silence. He starts crying and pushes away from them. Goes to the staffroom door, about to knock.*)

FOURTH BOY: Just you dare!

(*The* NEW BOY *hesitates, then turns in tears away from the door. Goes off as the others make their way through the side of the auditorium.*

In the staffroom, MRS SWIFT *is standing in front of* MR WRIGHT. *She begins slowly to walk around him. He begins to follow her in his chair.*)

MRS SWIFT: And tell me, how did this happen, Mr Wright?
MR WRIGHT: I do wish you would follow the children's example and call me Ro—
MRS SWIFT: *How did it happen?*
MR WRIGHT (*jumps. So does his chair*): I er . . . don't actually know. It was the end of the lesson, and I was sort of hopping about trying to collect in all the books, you know how one does . . . and . . . and the next thing I knew, I sat down and . . . well . . . there I was . . .

MRS SWIFT: Have you any concept, *Mr Wright*, of the damage that you are doing? Aren't you aware of the consequences of your actions? Do you actually realise what is happening – not just to you yourself, but to the school?

MR DEAN: Steady on, Freda . . .

MR WRIGHT: I am perfectly . . .

MRS SWIFT: Every Friday, I have to take a class of yours immediately after you have finished with them. Four days a week they come to me like little lambs. When they arrive after your lesson, they're mad dogs, foaming with excitement and looking for another victim. Now, why is that?

MR WRIGHT: Children often come away from my classes filled with excitement because I have stimulated them to new discoveries. (MRS SWIFT *closes her eyes*)

MR HADDOCK: Like finding out that wool and wood can be stuck together?

MR WRIGHT: Handy though, isn't it? You can sit down more or less wherever you want. (*He laughs*)

MR HADDOCK: Oh aye, marvellous. You should have a lot of fun driving home this afternoon. (*Turns away towards the tea-trolley*)

MR WRIGHT: I won't be going home straight away. I intend to join in the demonstration with Mr Dean.

MR HADDOCK: Well, there's another lost cause straight away, Graham.

MR WRIGHT (*goes to stand up. His chair comes with him and he stops*): Why do you . . .

MR HADDOCK: Yes?

MR WRIGHT: Nothing. (*Pause*) But with regard to this strike, speaking purely for myself . . .

MR HADDOCK: And may it always remain that way.

MR WRIGHT: *Look, can't you leave me alone?* (*This time he does stand*)

MR DEAN: You really are a bastard, aren't you, Haddock?

MR WRIGHT: From the first time I came in here, non-stop. All I want you to do is leave me alone. Can't you do that?

MR HADDOCK (*pause*): No. I can't help it. When I was a kid I used to drop cricket balls on ants. (*Turns back towards the teapot*) For hours on end I'd stand in our back yard ... (*Illustrates with the basketball*) 'Bumf, bumf, bumf, bumf, bumf ...' (*He puts the basketball on the trolley, takes hold of the teapot, finds that it is stuck, pushes it away*) It's got so lately that it's a disease. (*The TEA LADY comes down the corridor with another pot, enters*) I waste myself away killing ants, and keeping them in order. I come here five days a week, forty weeks a year, with no hope of a happy ending. (*He pours himself a cup of tea.* MRS SWIFT *stands and approaches the tea trolley.* MR DEAN *walks across as well.* MR WRIGHT *hesitates, then joins them. Stands near the tea trolley*)

MRS SWIFT: You should leave, you know that? You should.

MR HADDOCK: And where would I go? A thirty-eight-year-old PE teacher – they wouldn't interview me – they'd give me an MOT. (*Looks at her*) Anyway, what do you know that I should know?

MRS SWIFT: Nothing. I just think you would be better off. Quite a few of us would be. (*Again, she is very tired, and it shows in her movements*)

MR DEAN: Yeah, at least at another school we might get a few free periods.

MRS SWIFT: You're substituting for Miss Kite again next lesson? (*He nods*) Sorry about that, Graham. Maisie did do it last week.

MR DEAN: I'm used to it now. I'll take them up to the Art Room.

MR HADDOCK: Make a few more posters.

MR DEAN (*ignoring him*): Where is Maisie anyway? Is she all right today?

MRS SWIFT: Yes, at least, I think so, although you never know, not these days. She's on duty. Miss Kite's duty.

MR HADDOCK: What a woman. You know what her last doctor's note said – 'Terminal Hypochondria'.

MRS SWIFT: There's one in every school.

MR HADDOCK (*going away towards the chairs*): Oh well, roll on twelve o'clock.

MR DEAN (*coming forward hesitantly*): I'm hoping, actually, that most of you will join in with us on a demonstration at lunchtime, I think – we all think – that a show of strength, numbers, as many as possible, would be a great help. I don't want to go on about it ...

MR HADDOCK: Good. (*Quietly*) Bumf ... bumf ...

MR DEAN: ... but you all must realise that if we lie down and take it, they'll jump all over us for evermore.

MR WRIGHT: Hear, hear!

MR DEAN: I've had a really good initial response, there's going to be lots of us involved, I'm expecting most of the staff from the main school down here soon after twelve o'clock, and then we'll be straight across to the Education Office, catch them all coming out for lunch, and then down to the Town Hall. If you could put yourselves out for an hour or so ... (*Pause*) Look, you know, *it is important!* (*Silence*) Two of us are going to leave at Christmas. Forced to go – no choice in the matter. Doesn't that mean anything to you?

MR HADDOCK: Yeah, it means we'll have to fork out for two leaving presents.

MR DEAN: Oh, for Christ's sake! (*Silence.* DEAN *looks at them, looks at* WRIGHT, *who smiles encouragement at him*) You know, the longer I stay here, the more I despise you – all of your, four parts dead and nine tenths over thirty, sitting there stewing in your own juice, praying for a good pension and a lower mortgage rate ... (*Looks at* MRS SWIFT) ... chalk and talk and dead of heart, just doing the job for the fortnight in France, the extension to the house, the new car and the extra money. The money, the bloody money, how many of you actually *care*? Hey?

(*He has built himself up to screaming point. The* TEA LADY *is watching. The bell goes. He turns and walks out of the door.*
The TEA LADY *coughs. The others turn and look at her.*)

TEA LADY: Are you finished?

MR HADDOCK: Yes, I'm finished ... (*He sits there.* MR WRIGHT *goes over to the* TEA LADY *with his cup. He stands uncomfortably, looks at his timetable, fumbles with his chair, as the* TEA LADY *takes* HADDOCK's *and* MRS SWIFT's *cups*)

MRS SWIFT (*quietly. Warmly*): Come on, Don. Self-pity and cynicism isn't going to get you anywhere – only deeper into depression. Get any lower and you'll have to dig a hole.

MR HADDOCK: I know. But I've told you, I can't help it. Cynics are romantics at heart, you know. Failed romantics, tired of dreaming dreams that never come true. (*Pause*) Apart from killing ants, which I think perhaps came later, I spent a considerable amount of time as a child believing that I would be someone and do something ... (*American accent*) ... and make the world a better place to live in. That I'd fall in love, have children, teach well, do good, find a pattern and a purpose. Drive a straight line through life, somehow be sort of ... glittering. Not knowing that most of us work and worry and sweat and die unknown, and above all, alone. That humanity spends most of its time talking to itself. Or through its backside. (*He stands*) I have dribbled my life away, and I haven't even built an extension to my house. Even worse, it is a long time since I've done anything for anyone. I'm just hanging around, Freda, like most of us are. (*The first gang of pupils after breaktime come bursting down the corridor and off*) Listen to them, isn't it enough to hate them for? How can you 'care' for them when they're like that, young, happy, unknowing, not caring, and above all, ignorant. Jesus Christ, I envy them ... (*He walks towards the door as the* TEA LADY *goes out.* HADDOCK *crosses by where* WRIGHT *is standing, ready to go out to teach, chair and all.* HADDOCK *stops and looks at him. Flatly*) You're not going out there dressed like that, are you?

MR WRIGHT: I'm afraid I'm not in the habit of carrying a spare pair of trousers around with me.

(HADDOCK *laughs harshly.* WRIGHT *joins in eagerly with him, looks at* MRS SWIFT *for confirmation that he had made a joke.* HADDOCK *walks over to the pigeon holes, takes out his yellow track suit bottoms, throws them to* WRIGHT.)

MR HADDOCK: Here. (*Carries on towards the doorway*)
MR WRIGHT: Thank you ... thank you very much, Donald.

MR HADDOCK: It's nothing.
MR WRIGHT: Nevertheless ... (HADDOCK *goes out.* WRIGHT *holds the track suit bottoms, uncertain. Takes a step towards the door, turns back, looks at* MRS SWIFT. *She stands, takes some books and walks towards him*) Look, before you go ... (*She looks at her watch*) Yes, I know, you have a lesson, and so have I ... I just want to explain my purpose, I do have one ...
MRS SWIFT: Don't you think it would take too long?
MR WRIGHT: Can't you see, I am trying very hard? (*We hear a slow build-up of noises as the scene develops, starting now with some isolated whoops and shouts*)
MRS SWIFT: Effort alone is not enough, Mr Wright. And neither are good intentions. What matters is being able to carry them out.
MR WRIGHT: You don't want me here, do you? I can tell. You'd like to get rid of me.
MRS SWIFT: That is not for me to say. The Headmaster makes those kinds of decisions and we often differ considerably in our viewpoints.
MR WRIGHT (*blundering on*): He understands me, you see, whereas you ... no, I mean ...
MRS SWIFT (*turning away*): Come Christmas, Mr Wright, you won't have to worry any more about me.
MR WRIGHT: How do you ... (*Grabs her arm*) That's not fair, you can't redeploy me, not now, not yet ...
MRS SWIFT: That's not what I meant at all. Now, if you don't mind ...
MR WRIGHT: Please, Freda, I do have something to offer. I know I have. Come and see this lesson. This lesson, it's going to be very good ...
MRS SWIFT: It's very difficult. I have a class ...
MR WRIGHT: Look, I couldn't go through all this again, you can't get shot of me like that.
MRS SWIFT: If you would just listen ...
MR WRIGHT: *Please come.*
MRS SWIFT: I might, I'll ...
MR WRIGHT: Good, good, I know you'll be ...

Act Two

MRS SWIFT: I said I might. It depends on my class. (*They are both at the door. The noise is getting worse*)

MR WRIGHT: It's just a case of weathering the storm.

MRS SWIFT (*releasing herself*): It sounds to me as though the storm is approaching again, Mr Wright. I would go and face it if I were you. But I would change my trousers first. (*She turns coldly away from him, goes up the corridor.* WRIGHT *comes out into the corridor, looks towards front stage right, where some of his class now appear. We see that they are the boys who were involved with the* NEW BOY.)

FIRST BOY: Come on, Ron, we're all waitin' for you here.

FOURTH BOY: Come 'head, turn around an' let us have a look at y'.

FIRST BOY: Someone said you'd been through a sticky patch, Ron.

(*Laughter.* WRIGHT *ducks back into the staffroom, leans against the door. His considerable nerve is going on him. He begins to take his trousers off at a frantic pace. He gets the legs of the chair mixed up with his own legs.* MISS McKENSIE *comes down the corridor, goes to walk into the staffroom. As she goes between the boys at the staffroom door, they move away for her.*)

FOURTH BOY: Come on, boys, show a bit of respect.

(*They salute her. She gives a regal wave. They laugh.* WRIGHT *half stops the door, but not enough. She enters, looks at him, his trousers around his ankles, his hands between his legs.*)

MR WRIGHT: Now I can explain ... (*He begins to pull his trousers back on. She walks past him, as if dreaming. Stops and looks back*) No, you see, it was all good-natured, accidental almost, a small misfortune, easily rectified but rather wearisome, must dash, I have a class. (*He starts for the door. As he does so, the boys at the door start banging, stamping and shouting for him to hurry up. He turns back to* MISS McKENSIE) I have to ... I want to change my trousers. Maisie, I can't ... it would be wiser if ...

MISS McKENSIE: Your underpants don't interest me in the slightest.

MR WRIGHT: Ah, goo—

MISS McKENSIE: And neither do their contents. (*Smiles at him. Manic edge*)

MR WRIGHT: Oh ... er ... (*Goes to open the door. A few inches*)

BOYS: Wha–heh! Here he is. (WRIGHT *slams the door again.* HADDOCK *appears down stage right, advances quietly into the corridor towards the lads*)

FOURTH BOY: What're y' doin' in there, Ron?

MR WRIGHT: Excuse me, Miss ... (*Begins to take his trousers down again, equally as furiously, equally awkward*)

FOURTH BOY (*having shaken the doorhandle, now peeps through the keyhole*): What're we doin' t'day? It's not prejudice again, is it? (HADDOCK *is right behind him*) I'm fed up with prejudice, Sir. I'm prejudiced against it. (*The other three boys are aware of* HADDOCK. *They start coughing and nudging the* FOURTH BOY) We won't mess around if y'tell us about the birds an' the bees an' all that. 'Ey, Sir, is it true havin' a baby's somethin' t'do with Stork ... (*Looks around to the others, turns back*) ... margar ... (*Looks around again, stands up fast*) ... ine.

MR HADDOCK: The four of you, outside your classroom, in line, now. And not another word.

FOURTH BOY: We were only ...

MR HADDOCK: I said now, and I'll see you, Pembroke, as soon as the lesson's finished, outside my room. (*They turn away.* HADDOCK *turns towards the auditorium – he has his back to the boys. They flick 'V's at him*)

MR WRIGHT (*from the staffroom, where he is now in his underpants about to put on track suit bottoms*): Thank you, Mr Haddock, I'll be along in a moment. (*As he talks* HADDOCK *half turns to listen, almost catches the four boys as they, in unison, flick the 'V's. All in turn pretend to flick at their hair, scratch their head, pull at the sleeve of their jacket, and yawn –* HADDOCK *lets them get past. The* FIRST BOY *is nervous about going past him.* HADDOCK *raises his hand. The* FIRST BOY *ducks,* HADDOCK *flicks through his own hair. Smiles thinly at the* FIRST BOY. *They go off*) ... You know, I think things might be improving, Maisie. For the first time, just now, Mr Haddock, when I was stuck ... in difficulties, he helped me out. The very first time. I've always believed that things get better, you know. It is my philosophy in life. 'This Too Shall Pass.' And it will. (*Pause. He looks ludicrous in the tight bottoms*) I know it will. (*He opens the door with a brave flourish, starts off down the corridor as* MISS McKENSIE *speaks*)

MISS McKENSIE (*a variety of voices*): ... 'Things will get better' ... oh indeed ... 'This too shall pass' ... absolutely ... 'Life goes on, Maisie ...' ... of course ... 'You're a strange girl, Maisie, if you weren't my own daughter' ... Naturally ... 'Daddy, daddy ...' 'I watched my breasts form with the most bitter sense of disappointment, daddy. As if they were two tumours ...' (*Strident, sitting very erect*) There is no one else to talk to ... no one left who understands ... (*Then vaguely*) ... Rose ... Rose ... I can see things ... (*Laughs, stops*) ... but then they go away ... but one thing remains ... one thing stays ... one thing left to fight for ... *him*. I want him ... I want him ... seen through ... and gone ... before I ... (*Pause*)

(*We hear more voices coming from the area stage right of the auditorium. Enter* WRIGHT *with an uruly procession of pupils behind him – a 'ROSLA' class of at least fifteen. More boys than girls, perhaps.*

Throughout the scene that follows outside the staffroom door the FIRST BOY *attempts to stick an ass's tail on* WRIGHT'*s backside. He never quite succeeds, and as this is instant glue he has to keep smearing more on.*)

FIRST BOY (*manoeuvring around behind* WRIGHT): Are y'sure y'not goin' f'another cross–country run, Sir?
MR WRIGHT: No, now, I must insist ... quiet now, please, whoever it was who glued the door to the frame, I want you to ... (*Cries of 'It wasn't us' ... 'Honest' ... 'We wouldn't miss your lesson for the world' ... etc. etc.*)
LURCH (*steps forward. No menace other than his size*): I'll kick the door down for y', Ron. Smack, butt, wallop, just like that, no messin', no problem.
MR WRIGHT: Er, no thank you ...
FOURTH BOY: He doesn't believe y'can do it, Lurch.

LURCH: Wha'? Don't y'believe me, Sir? 'Ey? I'm hard I am, Sir. Aren't I?

MR WRIGHT: Yes well ...

FOURTH BOY: Offer him out, Sir, go on. I bet y'can't beat him. (*The* FOURTH BOY *pushes* LURCH *towards* WRIGHT *just as the* FIRST BOY *is attaching the tail to him.* LURCH *pulls away from* WRIGHT, *they all laugh as* WRIGHT *flaps, but the* FIRST BOY *gets hold of the* FOURTH BOY, *pushes him angrily away*)

FIRST BOY: Stupid. I had him then.

FOURTH BOY (*very defensively*): Sorry Loggo, I didn't know ...

MR WRIGHT: Enough ... now enough. Britton, show me you have brains as well as brawn. (LURCH *moves forward*) Firstly, find Mrs Swift and tell her that I have no classroom at the moment and could she come down if possible, and then find the caretaker for me, would you? Tell him the door is stuck, Britton. Ask him to come and release it.

LURCH: Oh yeah. (*Goes off up the corridor quickly*)

(*At this point, most of the class are noisy but within the bounds of school law and order. Some of them just stand and watch, disinterested, ready to go along with anything. One boy stands reading a paperback. Follows whatever movements occur, but lost in the novel. He has blue eyes.*)

FIRST GIRL: Ah come on, Sir. It's borin' out here. I want t'sit down.

SECOND GIRL: An' me.

MR WRIGHT: We won't be too long ...

FIRST GIRL: Why can't we go in another classroom?

MR WRIGHT: Because there are no other classrooms.

FIRST GIRL: I don't like standin' up.

SECOND GIRL: Neither do I.

FOURTH BOY: Why don't y'come an' lie down with me?

FIRST GIRL: Ah sod off.

MR WRIGHT: Now now, come on come on, let's just wait quietly till Britton returns.

FOURTH BOY: Ah, go on, Jackie, me an' you, 'ey, wha'd'y'say? (*Hand on her shoulder*)

FIRST GIRL: I said sod off! (*He persists, tries to put his arm around her*) Is that a shirt or have y'just been sick? ... Gerroff ... Sir, he's molestin' me.
MR WRIGHT: Now really, this has gone too far, Pembroke ...
FOURTH BOY: I haven't even got t'first base yet ...
FIRST BOY: Put her down, Pammo. (*Pause. Silence.* PEMBROKE *obeys. The* GIRL *smiles*) Y'don't know where she's been.
FIRST GIRL: An' you sod off an' all.
MR WRIGHT: I will not stand for such ...
FIRST BOY: 'Ey, Ron, why can't we go in there? (*Points to the staffroom*)
MR WRIGHT: No, it's ...
FIRST BOY: Ah, go on ...
SECOND BOY: Yeah ...
FOURTH BOY: It's big enough ...
MR WRIGHT: No, I can't poss—
FIRST BOY: Ah, y'all the same, you teachers. Promises an' preachin', all mouth an' miracles, an' nothin' ever happens.
FOURTH BOY: You said we was havin' a special lesson t'day ...

(*The noise increases again – lots of pushing and shoving.*)

MR WRIGHT: If you could just be quiet for a moment, and let me think ...

(*The* FIRST BOY *starts to approach* WRIGHT *again.*)

FIRST BOY: If y'don't do somethin' soon, Ron, there's goin' t'be trouble here.
SECOND GIRL: How d'you know?
FIRST BOY (*with menace*): 'Cos I'm goin' t'start it.
MR WRIGHT: I must have assurances from you, 5S, that you will be on your very best behaviour, otherwise ...
FIRST BOY: Oh we will, Ron ...
SECOND BOY: Scout's honour.
FOURTH BOY: Spit on the Bible.
THIRD BOY: Cross me heart an' hope t'die.
MR WRIGHT: Very well, then, I'll see what I can do.

(*Several whoops and shouts. They all bunch together behind him, the protagonists first, the more studious ones last, especially the boy with the book. Most of the class still have some vestige of self-discipline. It is important to note that this class, with two exceptions —* FIRST *and* FOURTH BOYS *— would give many other teachers no problem and some joy.*

WRIGHT *enters the staffroom. Approaches* MISS McKENSIE. *Some of the boys follow, and the two girls.* WRIGHT *turns back to them.*)

MR WRIGHT: Wait outside the room please. (*Not much authoirty, but the* FIRST BOY *leads the way out.* MISS McKENSIE *stands, behind* WRIGHT's *back, orders the kids out — points at the door.* WRIGHT *thinks he has been obeyed — turns to* MISS McKENSIE *to see if she has noticed. She sits quickly. Looks away*) Er, excuse me, Maisie, but a slight problem has arisen. The er door to Room 12 seems to be a trifle stuck. Nothing lasting, I'm sure. (*Glances at his pants and the chair, still firmly stuck together*) However, I am temporarily without a classroom, and I wondered if . . . you know, I could use the staffroom until the caretaker arrives.

MISS McKENSIE: The caretaker?

MR WRIGHT: Yes. I have sent for him. He won't be long.

MISS McKENSIE: Ah, good.

MR WRIGHT: I would imagine . . . it will only be . . . you know. (*He looks at his watch, looks at* MISS McKENSIE. *No hint of a reply*) Hmmm. So you have no objections? None at all? You're quite happy with the arrangements? (*Pause*) Good, good. (*Quietly, in confidence*) I think you might enjoy the lesson actually, when you find out what it's all about. (*Turns away, goes towards the door, opens it*) Right, in you come. (*Some rush in, others drift in. The leaders start investigating everywhere — most pupils never get inside the staffroom*) Now, can I remind you of your promise to . . . Pembroke, get rid of Mrs Swift's lunch, right now . . . (PEMBROKE *passes the sandwiches around. The* FIRST GIRL *moves towards the chairs. There are cries of* 'All right, Miss' *when they see* MISS McKENSIE) Jacqueline, not over there, please . . .

FIRST GIRL: I have t'sit down, Sir. Just f'a minute.

Act Two

MR WRIGHT: Yes well, just a minute then ... the rest of you ... (*The* SECOND GIRL *heads for the chairs*) Now Helen, not you as well ...

SECOND GIRL: Arrey ... (*But she stops*)

FIRST GIRL: But you said ...

MR WRIGHT (*sweetly*): Yes, I know, but time marches on, and if I waited for you to rest your lovely legs ... (*Wolf whistles and cries of 'Sir fancies y'' etc.*) ... not only would it be favouritism, but the lesson would be nearly over.

FIRST GIRL: But I'm talkin' t'Miss, aren't I, Miss? (*Pause*) Hello Miss. (*No answer*)

MR WRIGHT: Well, if you'll all gather around. (*One of the boys is standing on the table with an umbrella up, singing 'Singing in the Rain'*) For goodness sake, Williams, put that umbrella down ... Jacqueline, come on Jacqueline, there's a good girl ...

FIRST GIRL: It's nice in here, isn't it, Miss? Cosy like. (*Puts her feet up on the coffee table*)

MR WRIGHT (*as the majority of them gather around him*): Now, in a way I'm glad that Room 12 is er temporarily erm unavailable, because we need, in this particular lesson, room to express ourselves and ...

FOURTH BOY: I bet it's prejudice again, y'know ...

MR WRIGHT: Be quiet, now listen ...

FOURTH BOY: That's all we've ever done.

MR WRIGHT: This lesson is different, if only you'd ...

FOURTH BOY: I'm not prejudiced, I just hate all the blacks an' packies an' ...

MISS McKENSIE (*suddenly*): Shut up and grow up, you useless slimy little boy!

FOURTH BOY (*primly*): Yes Miss. (*Laughter*) Ah don't be like that, Miss. I was only ...

FIRST GIRL: You tell him, Miss.

MR WRIGHT: Indeed, I couldn't have put it better myself.

FOURTH BOY (*angrily*): Shut up, you, Ron. Don't *you* say anything t'me. You're soft.

MR WRIGHT: Now then, Pembroke, remember who you're talking to.

FOURTH BOY: I know who I'm talkin' to all right. (*Looks at* MISS McKENSIE, *then mutters*) Daft get . . . (*Silence*)

MR WRIGHT: Okay, fine, well done, at last some peace and quiet, perhaps now we can begin . . . Now then, hands up, how many of you were watching 'World in Action' last night. (*No one puts their hands up. One or two comments* – '*It's last, rubbish, we had the Bionic Man on' etc.*) None? Good, I thought as much. Now, there was a quite amazing discovery made on that programme by two scientists . . . (*More complaints: 'It's not a science lesson . . .' etc*) No, now listen, these two scientists have er scientifically proved that genetically speaking . . .

FOURTH BOY: Wha'?

FIRST BOY: Y'll get into trouble talkin' about genitals, Ron. Y'll be in the *News of the World*.

MR WRIGHT: No, genetics, the study of . . .

FIRST BOY: Genitals. Stands t'sense. Well, I'm not lettin' y'study mine.

MR WRIGHT: Genetics is the study of the origin of something. The growth.

FOURTH BOY: When y'rub mine it grows. (*Raucous laughter*) All right, Jackie?

FIRST GIRL: Isn't he dirty, Miss?

MR WRIGHT: I am talking about whole groups of people, Pembroke, and if you will let me finish, I will tell you something that will, quite frankly, amaze you.

FOURTH BOY: Oh go on then, I can hardly wait. (*Yawns loud and long*)

MR WRIGHT: These two scientists claim, and they have produced ample proof for their claim, that people with brown eyes are socially, physically and mentally superior to people with blue eyes.

FIRST BOY: Don't talk daft. (*General agreement*)

MR WRIGHT: It's not me, Logmond, it's these two scientists. They have proved it conclusively. Brown-eyed people are superior to blue-eyed people.

FIRST BOY: Load of cobblers.

Act Two

SECOND BOY: Yeah. (*The whole class start to furtively look at each others' eyes*)

FOURTH BOY: Oh aye, y'only sayin' that, you two, cos y've got blue eyes.

FIRST BOY: No I'm not.

FIRST GIRL: Hah hah, Loggo's inferior.

FIRST BOY: Shut it, you! You've got blue eyes as well.

FIRST GIRL: No they're not, they're sort of green. (*Cries of 'Blue Eye'* FIRST BOY *looks angrily around*)

MR WRIGHT: Nevertheless, it is my unfortunate duty to make sure that we brown eyes have as little contact as possible with the rest of you, and from now on in my lessons I will divide my class up into the clever intelligent virile brown eyes and the miserable stupid blue eyes.

SECOND BOY: You're mental.

MR WRIGHT: What is more, we shall treat you with the lack of respect that you deserve, and as far as I'm concerned, you are nothing more than mere animals, and to be trained as such.

FOURTH BOY: I always said you spoke sense, Ron. (*They are already breaking up into two camps*)

FIRST BOY: Anyone treats me like that, an' I'll treat them to a black eye, never mind a friggin' brown one.

FOURTH BOY: But you're inferior. Ron says so.

FIRST BOY: Sod Ron. Just you try it.

FOURTH BOY: An' anyway, there's more of us than you. (*Some agreement*)

MR WRIGHT: Come on, come on, line up, let me inspect you. (*The blue eyes are reluctant, stand at one side making their own group.* WRIGHT *starts inspecting the brown eyes, including the black boys and girls. One desperate blue-eyed girl tries to get into the brown eyes. The others shove at her.* WRIGHT *walks down the line, dismisses her from it. She rather sheepishly joins the other blue eyes. One or two still not involved, including* JACQUELINE *and the book-reader*) Good, good, well, it only leaves me to say that as from this moment, I consider the blue eyes to be nothing more than our slaves, mere lackeys within our power. We can do with them as we wish. Correct, brown eyes? (*This time some* enthusiasm in the agreement. But no action other than the clear formation of two camps)

FIRST BOY: Just you bloody well dare. Come on, you lot. (*The blue eyes come closer together*)

MR WRIGHT (*to the loner*): Jimmy ... Come on, Jimmy, join the rest of your rabble. (JIMMY *ignores* WRIGHT, *but the* FOURTH *and* THIRD BOY *look at him, whisper to each other*) Jacqueline, come on, Jacqueline. You've had a long rest now.

FIRST GIRL: I don't want to play. It's soft.

FOURTH BOY: 'Cos y'a blue eye!

FIRST GIRL: No, it's not. An' they're hazel, aren't they, Miss? (*Turns away from the others, opens her eyes wide for* MISS McKENSIE, *who nods*) There y'are, y'see.

MR WRIGHT: I tell you what, we'll make you an honorary brown eye, shall we? (*The start of cries of 'Suck-up' and 'Creep creep'. She hesitates*) Come on, Jacqueline, we'll give you the benefit of the doubt. How about that?

FIRST BOY: She's not brown-eyed, she's cross-eyed.

FIRST GIRL (*to* MISS McKENSIE): Why don't you play, Miss. You've got brown eyes, you join us.

MISS McKENSIE: No. Not just yet. (*She smiles*) Perhaps later.

MR WRIGHT: Over you come, Jackie, join Helen and the brown eyes. The superior brown eyes. (*She comes across. The blue eyes hiss her and make sucking noises*)

FOURTH BOY: Who're we goin' t'get then? (*No answer*) Look at them, yah, blue eyes, bomb heads.

SECOND BOY: You've had it outside, Pemmo.

FOURTH BOY: You an' who's army? We've got y' outnumbered, haven't we? (*General agreement.* WRIGHT *stands aside and watches, smiling happily*) Come on, let's get them, shall we? (*More agreement, but no advance. Some brown eyes are still nervous. The* FOURTH BOY *and the* THIRD BOY *mumble to each other again, slowly move over to the* LONER, *who is leaning against the pigeon holes with his paperback. The other brown eyes latch on, move across behind him. The* LONER *is unaware for some seconds, looks up, stares around, backs away into the pigeon holes*) Blue eye!

THIRD BOY: Bum.

Act Two

FIRST BLACK KID: Scum.
SECOND BLACK KID: Trash.
FOURTH BOY: Pig.
LONER: Wha'? Don't be daft. (*To* THIRD BOY) I'm your mate.
THIRD BOY: Not any longer, y'not. (*They are still only half serious*)
FOURTH BOY (*poking the* LONER): 'Cos you're inferior. Ron says so, an' he's our leader. But you're our slave, blue eye. You have t'do anythin' we tell y'.
LONER: Get lost.
FOURTH BOY (*still poking him*): Don't insult y'betters, Jimbo. Y'might not live t'tell the tale.
LONER: Leave me alone.
FOURTH BOY (*lifting up his foot*): My shoelace is undone. Tie it for me, blue eye.
LONER: Tie it y'self.
FOURTH BOY (*slaps him across the face. No force*): You do it, slave. (*Giggles and laughter from the brown eyes. The blue eyes are moved together by the* FIRST BOY)
FIRST BOY: Take no notice, Jimmy. (*The blue eyes huddle together. We see that the* FIRST BOY *is directing them*)
FOURTH BOY: Tie my shoelace, blue eye.
LONER: Won't.
FOURTH BOY (*snatches the book off him, passes it back to the* THIRD BOY *who throws it aimlessly over his shoulder*) I said tie it. (*He takes hold of his head, pushes it downwards. The* LONER *struggles*)
MR WRIGHT: Now, one thing I won't tolerate is physical violence, I should have ...

(*As he says this, the blue eyes rush forward, roaring like Red Indians, push* WRIGHT *aside, knock the brown eyes away, grab the* LONER, *bustle him back towards their territory. Shout and cheer. The brown eyes move across to them. The* FIRST BOY *takes hold of one of* MR DEAN's *signs, brandishes it in front of him threateningly.*)

FIRST BOY: Come on then, brown eyes, come on, let's see how superior y'really are. Suck this an' see wha' happens. (*He is in front of the other blue eyes, is clearly established as the leader*)

MR WRIGHT: Now now, Logmond, the purpose of this lesson . . .
FIRST BOY: You stay out of it, softarse.
MR WRIGHT: Logmond, now that is enough . . .
FIRST BOY: Enough — it hasn't started yet.
FOURTH BOY (*grabbing a pile of exercise books*): There's more of us than them — come on, what're we waitin' for? (*Starts to throw the books like frisbees at the blue eyes. The blue eyes retreat. More books are picked up by the brown eyes. The blue eyes return the fire. The* FIRST BOY *wildly waves the sign at the brown eyes, they move backwards. There is an uneasy truce.* WRIGHT *has spent his time flapping at the edge of the action*)
FIRST GIRL (*holding her face*): This is soft, I said it was.
MR WRIGHT (*moving into no man's land*): Good, good, now as I expected, once the blue eyes became victimised, they formed into a united front, one that cast aside all previous enmities and disputes, even to the point of rescuing Jimmy here, a gesture indeed quite noble and . . .
FIRST BOY (*leaning on the sign*): What is this — half-time?
MR WRIGHT: No, you see, another interesting factor in situations like this, is the inevitable emergence of a leader amongst the minority group. And, quite naturally, one such figurehead made his presence felt in this confrontation. (*Looks around. He is pleased with himself*)
FIRST BOY: Wha'?
MR WRIGHT (*approaching him*): You, Logmond, you became the leader of the oppressed minority. You took it upon yourself to make a stance, gather your forces, organise and administ—
FIRST BOY: I was just lookin' f'lumber.
MR WRIGHT: Ah, *you* might think that . . . (*Puts his arm around him. The* FIRST BOY *looks at his arm, looks at him, looks at the others, grins at the blue eyes*)
FOURTH BOY: He fancies you, blue eye.
FIRST BOY: Make the most of this, Pemmo, 'cos as soon as the bell goes, you'll be talkin' through yours. (*Shrugs* WRIGHT *away*)
MR WRIGHT: As I was saying, Logmond, you might think — you might like to think — that your actions were purely brutal and self-seeking, but I know better. Now, let me put this to you.

(Takes hold of his arm, moves him away from both camps)
FIRST BOY: Get off.
MR WRIGHT: No, listen, please, please listen. Your strength and leadership have impressed me very much. Genetically speaking, I think there must have been a mistake. You show every symptom of being a brown eye ...
THIRD BOY: We wouldn't have him! (FIRST BOY *turns angrily, points, then turns back*)
MR WRIGHT: Now, as before with Jacqueline, I have it in my power to make you into an honorary brown eye. You can go over there, and be one of us. Superior in every way. Special, Logmond. Better than the blue eyes.
FIRST BOY (*glances at the blue eyes*): Leave them?
MR WRIGHT: They don't deserve you, Logmond. A boy of your qualities ...
FIRST BOY: Y'really think I should be, like, y'know, a brown eye?
MR WRIGHT: Of course I do.
FIRST BOY: But d'y'reckon I'll be good enough? Y'know, if they really are better than us blue eyes, I mean ...
MR WRIGHT: You have nothing to worry about, I assure you.
FIRST BOY (*coyly*): I er dunno ...
MR WRIGHT: This is your golden opportunity, Logmond.
FIRST BOY: I don't want t'tell you in front of all these, Sir. Y'know ... (*Looks at the blue eyes sheepishly*)
MR WRIGHT: Of course, of course, I quite understand. (*Leads him further forward*)
FIRST BOY (*looking around*): D'y'mind if I whisper in y'ear, Sir?
MR WRIGHT: No, that's quite all right. Very sensitive of you.
FIRST BOY (*leaning up towards* WRIGHT): Fuck off, Sir!

(*Laughter. The* FIRST BOY *darts back towards the blue eyes, picks up a book, hurls it across. More books fly between both camps. Plus anything else handy. The contents of the pigeon holes.* WRIGHT *runs around in circles and into the middle. Gets his fair share of missiles. We see the* CARETAKER *and* BRITTON *come into the corridor.*)

MR WRIGHT: No, no, stop, now you've gone too far ... ow!

(The CARETAKER and BRITTON advance. The carnage continues, with the FIRST BOY grouping his troops at one end of the staffroom, while the brown eyes are nearest the door. Some are still not enthusiastic, but are chivvied along by the FOURTH and THIRD BOYS.)

CARETAKER *(at the doorway)*: Your class an' him deserve each other, d'y' ... *(Enters)* What the bloody hell ... *(Moves into the room, surveys the scene and dodges the missiles. Slowly, they all stop)*

MR WRIGHT: Ah, thank you, Britton.

LURCH: Mrs Swift said she'd try and get down in a few minutes.

MR WRIGHT: Good, well done. *(He approaches the CARETAKER and BRITTON, and makes a great play of looking into BRITTON's eyes)* Yes, brown, I should have guessed, over you go. *(Points towards the brown eyes. BRITTON looks bewildered but goes. MISS McKENSIE is no longer facing front. She looks across at the CARETAKER)*

CARETAKER: You wouldn't like to tell me what's goin' on here, would you, Mr Wright.

MR WRIGHT: It's quite simple really. The door to Room 12 has ...

CARETAKER: I already know that. Mastermind's just told me. *(BRITTON looks across at him, goes to move forward, stops)* It's here that interests me. My cleaners are on their knees every morning cleaning this place. Making it nice for the staff, spotless, spick an' span, a sanctuary. Not a battlefield, Mr Wright, for you an' these delinquents here ... *(MISS McKENSIE stands, advances)*

FOURTH BOY: 'Ey, watch who you're callin' names, you.

THIRD BOY: Or y'might end up on the ceilin' with y'bike. *(Laughter)*

CARETAKER: I knew as bloody much ...

FOURTH BOY: Ah, go an' play with y'Windolene.

LURCH: Mop-head. *(More laughter)*

CARETAKER: Don't talk t'me like that, just don't ... *(MISS McKENSIE stands between him and the brown eyes)*

MISS McKENSIE: I think I might just want to play now.

Act Two

CARETAKER: Oh, I should have known you'd have somethin' t'do with it. Right bloody pair you two make. Well, we'll see about this ... (*Half turns, sees that the brown eyes are between him and the door*)
MISS McKENSIE (*as he turns back, inspects his eyes*) Blue eye. (*Pokes him*) Blue ... eye.
CARETAKER: 'Ey no, don't you touch me ...
MR WRIGHT: I think we're all gettin' carried away. I suggest ...
FOURTH BOY: Yeah, *blue eye*.
LURCH: Puddin' brain. (*Pause*) Er, what's goin' on?
CARETAKER: I hope you're remembering all this, Mr Wright, 'cos ...
MISS McKENSIE: Scum.
CARETAKER: I beg your pardon?
MISS McKENSIE: Scum.
CARETAKER: Oh.
THIRD BOY: Trash.
FOURTH BOY: Slime.
FIRST BLACK KID: Monkey face.
CARETAKER: Will someone tell me what's ...

(*The brown eyes start moving towards him. For the first time they are all enthusiastic, jeering, shouting. WRIGHT is having a canary fit.*

We see MRS SWIFT come down the corridor. Her pace quickens as she hears the noise. She enters the room, sees the pupils about to converge on JACKSON.)

MRS SWIFT: What on earth's going on? (*She looks at* WRIGHT)
MR WRIGHT (*as the pupils carry on, either not noticing* MRS SWIFT *or ignoring her*): This wasn't meant to ... I can assure you ...
MRS SWIFT: 5S ... 5S ...
MR WRIGHT (*at her side*): Go back ... go back ...
MRS SWIFT: Stop it this minute ... (*One or two stop – perhaps the girls*) 5S!
FIRST BLACK KID: Y've always hated us.
SECOND BLACK KID: Treated us like dirt.

CARETAKER: Don't be so ...
FIRST BLACK KID: Told us t'stop givin' you black looks.
SECOND BLACK KID: Then laughed.
MRS SWIFT (*near to them*): Stop this behaviour at once.
MR WRIGHT: Yes.
CARETAKER: Mrs Swift ...
FIRST BLACK KID: An' all the time, little old blue eyes, we were better than you.
SECOND BLACK KID: Cos we've got brown eyes.
FOURTH BOY: Hit him, Hovis, I would ...
MRS SWIFT (*stands between the* CARETAKER *and the pupils*): Now that will be all ...
MR WRIGHT (*following her*): I made it up, I made it up, can't you see, they're all the same, blue and brown ... (*Turns to* MRS SWIFT) ... it was just a lesson, that's all ... (*Turns to the pupils*) Prejudice, Pembroke, prejudice, see, that's all it was ...
FIRST BLACK KID: An' he knows all about that.
MRS SWIFT: Whatever it was ...
MISS McKENSIE: Fascist!
SECOND BLACK KID (*along with others*): Yeah, Fascist!
SEVERAL: 'Seig Heil, Seig Heil ...'
MRS SWIFT: For God's sake ...
MISS McKENSIE (*slowly, stressing every syllable*): Mem ... ber of ... the ...
CARETAKER: Ratepayers' Association!
MISS McKENSIE: Nat ... ion ... al ... Front!
MRS SWIFT: Maisie! (*Tries to take hold of her, is pushed away*)
FIRST BLACK KID: Nazi! (*Pushes the* CARETAKER *hard*)
CARETAKER: The Headmaster'll hear of this ... (*Laughter from the pupils.* MRS SWIFT *looks at them. Stops*)
MR WRIGHT: Boys, boys ...
FIRST BLACK KID: Blue eye ...
THIRD BOY: Bastard.
FOURTH BOY (*pushes the* CARETAKER *as well*): Blue-eyed bastard.
CARETAKER: Mrs Swift ...
MR WRIGHT: Please stop them, Mrs Swift. (*She just stares at them*)
CARETAKER (*as they crowd around him, poking him, jeering*): Get the

Act Two

Headmaster ... (*More jeers*) Get off! Get away! (*Waves his fist at them*) You won't dare do anything, you don't scare me, I've got a position here.

(*The* FOURTH BOY *raises his fist as* HADDOCK *did to him earlier. The* CARETAKER *ducks away, half falls, half turns into the crowd of blue eyes. He falls against the* FIRST BOY.)

FIRST BOY (*as he violently shoves the* CARETAKER *away*): Well, that's one blue eye I'm not rescuin'.

(MR DEAN *comes into the corridor with some more posters. He moves towards the staffroom door, enters as the* CARETAKER *spins into the empty space near the back wall and the record player.* WRIGHT *is at* MRS SWIFT's *elbow.*)

MR WRIGHT: Mrs Swift ... *Mrs Swift*, you can stop her, you can stop them ... please.

(*She looks at him, looks at the rest of them, turns away towards the chairs as the* CARETAKER *speaks.*)

CARETAKER (*points at* MISS McKENSIE): It's you ... it's you, it's not me, Mrs Swift ... Mrs Swift, it's them, it's her, she's incitin' this lot, she's makin' them do it ... (*The pupils are slowly surrounding him. He sees* MR DEAN *at the door*) Ah, Mr Dean, of course, oh yes, why not? It's a plan, they've organised it. I should have guessed ... get away from me, don't get any nearer, stay away, filth ... (*They are in a circle around him.* DEAN *approaches*) Garbage. (*The pupils start hissing him*) Animals. (*They start mooing*) Look at you, just look at you, y'only provin' our point, black trash an' gutter scum.

(*One of the black kids grabs him and throws him into the circle. He is hurled around the circle as* MR DEAN *runs forward, breaks the circle and pushes him away. The* CARETAKER *sprawls onto the ground.* DEAN *looks at the group. At first they do not move, then slowly edge away.*)

MR DEAN: What is this? What's going on? *Well?*

79

(*The* NEW BOY *comes running into the corridor, into the staffroom.*)

NEW BOY (*holding a note*): Sir, Mr Dean, Sir ...
MR DEAN: Not now, boy ...
NEW BOY: But the Head—
MR DEAN: Just wait ... See Mrs Swift (*He looks across at her. She ignores him*)
NEW BOY: The Headmaster wants to see ...
MR DEAN: *Not now!* (*Points to where the blue eyes are*) Wait over there. (*The boy looks across. The* FIRST BOY *smiles at him, beckons him across. The* NEW BOY *goes over nervously*) Will someone tell me what's happening? Joey ... Jimmy ... Dave ... Lurch ... Helen ... Jackie ... (*They refuse to look at him*) Why?
CARETAKER: I'll tell y' wh—
MISS McKENSIE (*manically thrusting himself in front of him*): What does it feel like to be inferior?
MR DEAN: Maisie, come away ... (*Tries to take hold of her, grabs her, they struggle, he looks at* MRS SWIFT) Freda, f'Christ's sake, don't just sit there. (MISS McKENSIE *ducks away from him*) What's *happening?*
MISS McKENSIE: How do you like being picked on, picked out and reviled, told you're different to others, cast off, cast out, not as good as the rest of us? (DEAN *takes hold of her from behind. She is frenzied. The kids still surround the* CARETAKER) What's it like knowing you're despised and hated, looked down upon, blue eye? Nazi, Fascist, Memb ... Memb ... member ... (*She turns away, head down, sobs wildly. The* CARETAKER *laughs loudly*)
FOURTH BOY: Don't you laugh at her, you!

(*The* THIRD BOY *picks him up, throws him into the crowd. They converge on him, surround him. Many of the blue eyes go across. We see that the* FIRST BOY *stays, watches the action, then takes out of his pocket the donkey's tail, puts his arm around the* NEW BOY. MR WRIGHT *tries to reach the* CARETAKER. MR DEAN *leaves* MISS McKENSIE, *who slowly moves towards the chairs.* MRS SWIFT *has put her hands over her eyes.* MR DEAN *drags the* CARETAKER *out of the mêlée. He is bleeding from the nose. Although rescued by* DEAN, *he instantly pushes him away, backs towards the door.*)

FIRST BOY (*a harsh whisper*): Go on. (*We see him push the* NEW BOY *hard towards the* CARETAKER. *The* BOY *stops, looks around, the* FIRST BOY *threatens him, he ventures slowly forward*)
CARETAKER: Yes, come on, come on, hit me, punch me, kick me, put me in hospital, go on, go on, every attack brings publicity, publicity brings recruits. It won't be long now, we won't need the voting booths, we'll have the streets, and then we'll have the power. See what happens then, Dean. See who gets beaten up *then*. (MR DEAN *gets hold of him*) Oh yes, that's right, don't stop them, join them, make a meal of it. Here, just here. (*Offers his face.* DEAN *stops, pauses, then releases him*)
FIRST BLACK KID: Don't worry, we'll get him for y', Sir.
MR DEAN (*quietly*): No, no, I don't believe in violence.
CARETAKER: Fool. Fool. (*The* FIRST BOY *is now pushing the* NEW BOY *towards the* CARETAKER)
MR DEAN: Violence is the last act of the defeated mind. (*He turns away, faces front, does not see the* NEW BOY)
CARETAKER: You'll never get anywhere then. Nowhere. (*Grabs hold of one of* DEAN's *posters on the floor*) Words. Just words. (*Throws it away*)

(*The* NEW BOY *is creeping slowly behind the* CARETAKER *with the donkey tail.* WRIGHT *has turned away towards* DEAN. *The* NEW BOY *gets closer, attempts to put the tail on the* CARETAKER. *He feels the lad's clumsy efforts, turns, grabs the tail, grabs the* BOY, *hits him across the head and throws him away. Before the* BOY *has landed, he is screaming. As he lands, he goes into an epileptic fit. The pupils leap away from him, then advance. The screams bring* MRS SWIFT *to her feet.* MR WRIGHT *flaps,* MR DEAN *grabs the* CARETAKER, *pushes him away, goes to the* BOY, *joined by* MRS SWIFT, *tries to control him.*)

MR DEAN (*to the pupils*): Get away, get away! (*They retreat*)
CARETAKER (*on the floor*): It wasn't my fault, I didn't know …
MRS SWIFT: His tongue. His tongue.
MR DEAN: But what do I do?
MR WRIGHT (*near hysterical – almost an excuse to get out*): I'll call an

ambulance. (*Gets to the door as* MR HADDOCK *walks from the gymnasium, stage right*)

(WRIGHT *goes to run up the corridor, sees* HADDOCK.

MR WRIGHT: Mr Haddock! Mr Haddock! Donald . . . Quick quick!

(HADDOCK *runs into the staffroom.* WRIGHT *scuttles after him. He is breaking up.* DEAN *is trying to stop the boy jerking,* MRS SWIFT *is with him.* HADDOCK *pushes them both away.*)

MR HADDOCK: Leave him! Let him do it . . .

(HADDOCK *undoes the* BOY's *shirt collar.* MR WRIGHT *is crying,* MISS McKENSIE *is giggling very quietly,* MRS SWIFT *and* MR DEAN *stand above* HADDOCK. *The* CARETAKER *tries to get out, but is stopped silently by the pupils.* HADDOCK *forces his fingers down into the boy's throat, releases his tongue. He gets bitten for his efforts. It all takes time. The* NEW BOY *slumps, the spasms slow down then stop.* HADDOCK *looks at his hands, badly bitten. The class mumble. They all look at* HADDOCK.)

MR WRIGHT: Oh thank God, thank God . . .
MR DEAN: You saved him.
MR WRIGHT (*blubbering*): Yes . . . yes.
MR HADDOCK: I know. (*Turns to* MRS SWIFT, *smiles*) It was nothing. (*Stands up*) You, boy . . . (*Pause, then gently*) McKenna, secretary's office, an ambulance, lad, straight away. (McKENNA *is half way out of the door*) Hurry now.
McKENNA: Yes, Sir!
MR DEAN: We didn't know what to do.
MR HADDOCK: It was part of my training. That's all.
MRS SWIFT: Thank you, Don. (*Turns away*)
MR DEAN: Yeah . . . thanks.

(HADDOCK *nods, looks around the room, sees the chaos, sees the* CARETAKER *still surrounded, sees* MISS McKENSIE *and* MR WRIGHT *for the first time with clarity since he entered the room.*)

Act Two

MR HADDOCK: What happened?
FOURTH BOY: He hit him. (*He points to the* CARETAKER)
FIRST BOY: Yeah, that's right.
CARETAKER: It was all a mistake. I never meant ...
FIRST BLACK KID: Yes y'did.
LURCH: Y'did it on purpose. Blue eye.
SECOND BLACK KID: Nazi.
CARETAKER: Just you be careful, you ...
MR HADDOCK (*looks at* MRS SWIFT, *who shakes her head. She has had enough*) Just hang on a minute. (*He picks the* BOY *up*) Did you hit him?
CARETAKER: It wasn't quite like that. I just ... (*Waves his arm, as if he had merely brushed the* BOY *in passing with his hand*)
MR HADDOCK: *Did you hit him?*
CARETAKER: I ... look at my nose. Look. They ... I was attacked ... Yes.
MR HADDOCK: NF?
CARETAKER: Wha'? Who me?
MR HADDOCK: NF?
CARETAKER: Well, so what? I'm entitled to hold polit—
MR HADDOCK: Good-bye, Mr Jackson. (*Pause.* HADDOCK *advances towards the door with the* NEW BOY. *The* CARETAKER *and he face each other*) Good-bye.
CARETAKER (*laughs nervously*): Where am I going?
MR HADDOCK: Away. If you've got any sense.
CARETAKER: But ...
MRS SWIFT (*quietly, back turned*): You heard Mr Haddock.
CARETAKER (*plaintively*): But Mrs Swift ...
MR DEAN: The whole class saw you, the whole class heard you, and so did the senior mistress. It's not just the word of a mad member of staff now, Jackson. (*Looks at* MISS McKENSIE, *who stares out*)
CARETAKER (*as* HADDOCK *goes out of the door*): You don't know, Mr Haddock, you never saw what happened. It's a conspiracy ... (*The* CARETAKER *stands by the door*) It's them, it's her, that cow. (*Looks nervously at the class*) They made me do it.
MR HADDOCK: Get out. Now.

(*The* CARETAKER *turns back to the staffroom, looks at* MRS SWIFT, *then at the others. Sees* DEAN.)

CARETAKER: I'll see you on the streets. (*Some of the class move towards him, he ducks out and scuttles off*)

MISS McKENSIE: He . . . he won't see me. (*Pause.* HADDOCK *goes off with the* NEW BOY)

FIRST BOY: All right, Sir, Ron, we've had prejudice, book throwin', threatenin' behaviour, assault an' battery an' a course in life savin'. What's next? (*A few half-hearted laughs*)

MR DEAN: Some lessons in manners, Logmond.

FIRST BOY: O Level or CSE? (*To* WRIGHT) Got five minutes left, Ron. Easy slip in a few miracles or somethin'.

MR WRIGHT: Just leave me alone. That's all, leave me alone.

MR DEAN: Watch it, Logmond.

FIRST BOY: Why? What're you goin' t'do? You don't believe in violence. You just said so. You can't hurt me.

MR DEAN: What makes you such a bastard, Logmond? You and the others like you. You make me . . .

MRS SWIFT (*quietly, from a distance*): Leave it, Graham, it's not worth it.

MR DEAN: Oh yes it is. (*Turns again to* FIRST BOY) I can get through to nearly every kid in this school, but the likes of you, there's a brick wall around you. Starting at your brain.

FIRST BOY: That's what you think, softhead.

MR DEAN: Well come on then, enlighten me.

FIRST BOY: It's a different world where I come from, Dean. You've never had t'fight f'anythin' – or even want it, have y'? Have y'? (*Laughs*) I bet y've never known a need – never even been outside of school or university in y'life.

MR WRIGHT (*struggling not to cry*): But why do you have to fight us? Why do you do it? I've never been less than kind to you. I've tried to understand.

FIRST BOY: Kind? You're not kind, Ron. You're soft. (*He picks up* WRIGHT's *trousers, laughs. We hear the bell go*) Y'know what I've been brought up t'believe – 'The Meek Shall Inherit A Kick In The Bum'. Y'get what y'can out of this life, pal – an' y'dont' get nothin' unless y'fight for it. (*He goes towards the door*) Y'know me – I'm never goin' t'be less than happy all my life. (*He laughs. Humphrey Bogart*) So long, blue eyes.

(*The rest of the class drift out after him. Many are embarrassed. The girls are the last to go. The* FIRST *and* SECOND GIRLS *seem to want to say something, but fail to find the words.* HADDOCK *returns as* DEAN *talks.*)

MR DEAN: Slimy screwed-up get that he is, he's right. I've never had to fight for anything. I've been inventing them for years: leading a positive life, making my own beer, reading the *New Statesman* and supporting all the right causes ...

MR HADDOCK (*gently*): And what are the right causes, Graham?

MR DEAN (*snorts*): Where do you want me to start? Everything from being a vegetarian to believing in the comprehensive system. And Christ knows, I still believe in it. I mean, for fuck's sake, what is there if there's nothing decent and honourable to believe in?

MR HADDOCK (*puts his arm around him*): Very little, Graham. Not at your age. And who knows, perhaps you'll be one of those lucky ones who drives that straight line along the road. Perhaps, even, before you reach the end of it, you might just help to move the world, or one or two people, in the 'right' direction.

MR DEAN: But what about the caretaker? The likes of him, aren't they ... what can *I* do about them? Why do they exist?

MR HADDOCK: Your decency and my disinterest allow them to exist, old son. And for you, there's no other way.

MR DEAN: And what about you? (HADDOCK *laughs and turns away*) I've hated you ever since I came. You must know that.

MR HADDOCK (*turns back*): Oh aye. You had good reason. (*Grins*) And I'll probably give you more cause to, and all. Nobody changes Graham. Not overnight. A week next Monday morning you'll still be a liberal left-wing wet, and I'll still be bitter and twisted and a failure and a has-been. We'll still get up each other's noses, so let's not make friends, hey? (*Turns back towards the chairs*) There is no happy end.

MR DEAN (*grabs hold of him*): You saved that kid's life. I thought, just then, when it all happened, that ... that it touched you. You'd done something.

MR HADDOCK: I did what I was trained to do, Dean. And what I get paid five and a half thousand a year for. That's all.

MR DEAN: You're lying. I saw it.

MR HADDOCK: Well, *you* remember it then. (*Taps* DEAN *on the cheek twice, goes to move away*)

MR DEAN (*grabs him again, turns him violently*): For once in your soddin' life, Haddock, come out from behind that miserable cynical mask of yours. Come on, come on, older man, wiser man, you know everything – *tell me!*

MR HADDOCK: I've told you. Your decency and my disinter—

(DEAN *grabs him again.* HADDOCK *throws him away, grabs hold of one of* DEAN's *placards, goes after him, takes hold of* DEAN *by the scruff of his jacket with his free hand.*)

MR HADDOCK: You bloody immature pretentious little wet-arse, y'waving your placards while the slime rises out of the ground once again. Don't you know what you're up against – what good are words – what use is a slogan – when you're up against *them.* Six million dead, old son, that's what the National Front's heritage is – and you know why the Jews were goose-marched to the 'delousing units' – *because they represented someone to hate.* Oh, how we love someone to hate ... don't we, Dean? Divide and rule. (*Smiles at him, lets go of him*) And remember this – at almost any time before it was too late and he was in power, Hitler could have been crushed. But what happened – decent people like you allowed it to happen – stepped aside, Pontius Pilates with placards – while they made plans for hot and cold gas in the Auchwitz showers. (*Pause*) You, you didn't even know what was going on here till today, till it was spelt out for you. And you know why – cos you were locked up in your decency and fine words, and I think you always will be. (*Half turns away, then turns back*) But if you really want to fight the scum, and you've got nothing else left – (*Takes the placard, breaks it in two across his knee, holds out the bottom piece like a stave*) ... use this. (*Now turns away from him*)

MR DEAN: But ... but I can't.
MR HADDOCK: I know. And neither can I. But there might come a time when we have to.

(*He throws the stave away. Turns away towards the chairs.* DEAN *and* HADDOCK *face away from each other. Pause.* MR WRIGHT *coughs. Then coughs again.*)

MR WRIGHT: How ... how is the boy, Mr Haddock. Is he all right?
MR HADDOCK: Yes, he will be. But by some gross piece of misfortune, his mother had been kept waiting two hours by the Headmaster, and when she saw her little treasure, lovely middle-class lady that she is, she screamed blue murder ... consequences.
MR WRIGHT: Will that mean ... what will it do to me? It ... it was all my fault. It was, wasn't it? (*No answer*) No, don't argue with me, I know it was ... Freda, you said before about redeploy— ... (*Giggles suddenly*) ... and now this ... I'm finished. I didn't realise it was going to be like this. *I thought I'd win!* (*He too goes towards the easy chairs*)
MR HADDOCK: And before I forget, Graham, he wants to see you.
MRS SWIFT: The Head?
MR HADDOCK: Yes.
MR DEAN: Oh, that's what the message must have been about ... that boy ...
MRS SWIFT: Oh. (*Looks at* DEAN) Oh well.
MR DEAN: Do you know what he wants me for?
MRS SWIFT (*standing*): No, I don't *know*, and I don't want to know anymore. I should congratulate you, Graham. Your strike action was exquisitely timed, otherwise I would have had an afternoon of absolute hell.
MR DEAN: Yes. Strike action. (*Looks at his watch. Not a great deal of enthusiasm*) The others should be here now. Soon anyway. I'll go and see what the Head wants ...
MRS SWIFT: Deny ever seeing me, if he asks.
MR DEAN: Yeah ... look, when the others come, would you tell

them, you know ... wait for me, I won't be long ... (*Moves into the room again*) If you don't want to join in ... if it's difficult ... you know, what I'm trying to say is ... well ...

MR HADDOCK: We can have a Ploughman's Lunch at the Bow and Arrow and you won't sulk?

MR DEAN: Something like that. (*Turns and exits*)

MR HADDOCK: Well then. (*Turns towards* MISS McKENSIE) Maisie, a celebration lunch?

MISS McKENSIE: I don't want anything else. I'm going to close the door and never come out ever again.

MR HADDOCK (*gently*): Better leave a note for the milkman.

MISS McKENSIE: Daddy used to say that. (*She smiles*) Funny really, we lived on a farm ... (*Looks up at him*) Daddy?

MR HADDOCK (*turns away, closes his eyes briefly. Sighs*): Freda, then. Come on, anything you want, as long as it's a pork pie.

MRS SWIFT: Peach melba and raw carrots. I just fancy that. (HADDOCK *looks at her, looks down at her stomach*)

MR HADDOCK: With a lump of coal for pudding? (*She nods*) I don't think they serve that at the Bow and Arrow. Mothercare sell it in instant packets though.

MR WRIGHT (*the penny drops*): You mean you're ...

MRS SWIFT: Running away. (*She turns towards the door, then stops, turns back*)

MR WRIGHT: And I thought I was going to be re ... rede ... (*Stares ahead, vacantly*)

MR HADDOCK: So you finally did it. (*She nods*) Some women'd do anything for six months' paid leave. (*He smiles at her*)

MRS SWIFT: It wasn't really planned. It was an accident ... and until today I thought perhaps I would come back as soon as ... you know. But not now ... I've had enough. When I do come back into teaching, it'll be somewhere else ... no position. No power. No timetable. *And no idiot of a boss with a lifetime tenure.* What's more, I'll never let the likes of him shove me away in a wing where sheer survival keeps me out of harm's way. ... You know, all I needed was someone to look up to, someone I believed in in a position of power! The bastard.

MR HADDOCK (*arm around her*): Come on, let's go.

MRS SWIFT: I've gone already. I haven't even handed my notice in yet, I won't leave till Christmas, but I'm already not here... (*She looks across at* MISS McKENSIE, *goes across, kneels down*) I'm sorry, Maisie, you were right after all. I never gave you any time, did I? I just... I never seemed to have any, not with... (*She indicates the staffroom — the school.* MISS McKENSIE *stares ahead.* MRS SWIFT *stands.* HADDOCK *has moved towards the door*)

MR HADDOCK: You can bring the bottoms back on Monday, Mr Wright. (WRIGHT *doesn't hear him*) Ronald... *Ronald*. (WRIGHT *turns towards him*) It doesn't matter about the bottoms, okay? (WRIGHT *jumps up in his chair, stands quickly*)

MR WRIGHT: No, no, I might not see you... we might never... (*Giggles, starts taking the track suit bottoms off in a hurry.* HADDOCK *goes across*)

MR HADDOCK: But you need them... hey... you have to go home.

MR WRIGHT (*as he tugs the trousers off*): Here, here, here...

MR HADDOCK: Look, really, how are you...

(WRIGHT *thrusts them into* HADDOCK's *hands.* MRS SWIFT *stands by* HADDOCK, *facing* WRIGHT *in his underpants. She turns away, takes* HADDOCK's *arm.*)

MRS SWIFT: Come on, I don't want to stay, there's worse to come.

MR HADDOCK: How do you mean? (*He follows her with the track suit bottoms*)

MRS SWIFT: Nothing. I just don't want to be here when Graham comes back. (*Quickly*) What are you going to do with them at home?

MR HADDOCK (*pause. Then almost shyly*): I'm going to wash them. And then I'm going to bring them back and wear them.

(*He turns and goes out. She watches him and then follows him. They walk up the corridor and exit.*
As they go off, the CLEANER *comes from the auditorium area, stage right, with mop and bucket. Goes into the staffroom.* WRIGHT *and* MISS McKENSIE *are sitting side by side.*)

CLEANER: What a bloody shambles!

No More Sitting on the Old School Bench

(*She walks over, looking at the mess and tutting. Starts picking the books up, approaches* MR WRIGHT, *gets a book by his feet, looks up, sees his bare legs, follows the course of his legs up to his underpants, looks at him, starts backing away.*

We see MR DEAN *come into the corridor. Blank-faced, nearly stumbles, enters the staffroom, head down. Then, expecting a crowd, looks around.*)

CLEANER (*sweetly*): Mornin', Mr Dean.
MR DEAN: Mmm? Oh, mmm. (*To* MISS McKENSIE *and* MR WRIGHT) Have you seen the others? (*No answer*) Did they go on ahead? (*Still no answer*) Maisie . . . (*He looks around. Sees his signs*) Didn't anyone come? (*Pause*) Yeah . . . (*He walks towards the door, stops, turns back, picks up a signal, looks at it, holds it up, walks out of the staffroom, holding it as if in a march. Gets into the corridor. The* HEADMASTER *comes into the corridor*)
MR GRANT: Ah . . . yes . . . mmmm, I hope . . . (DEAN *walks straight past him.* GRANT *goes back after him*) Mr Dean . . . Mr Dean . . . (DEAN *goes off*) . . . I can understand how you . . . but my reference will be . . . (*The* HEAD *turns back towards the staffroom, enters, sees the mess, hesitates, looks at* MR WRIGHT *and* MISS McKENSIE. *Goes towards them. The* CLEANER *leans on her mop and watches*) Ah, well, amazing hey, another half term gone. (*Notices* MR WRIGHT *has no trousers, double takes, then determines not to bring it up*) One or two problems, but I am confident, yes, confident. All's well that ends well. I will, of course, want a written statement, Mr Wright, some details of the events, but I think we can find a way through . . . around . . . a worthy settlement . . . yes. And you, Miss McKensie, how is life with you? I was only thinking to myself this morning your examination results, we never seem to give you the credit they deserve . . . take it from me, we all . . . appreciate . . . we know . . . it goes without saying, but sometimes it does need saying . . . and so now I'm saying it. Yes. (*Stands*) Well. There you are. Must erm . . . must dash. You know. (*Turns away, goes past the* CLEANER) Lot's to be done, Mrs . . . Mrs . . . (*She does not hide her disregard*) Keep right on till the end of the road. (*He*

Act Two

is now fidgeting, touching things on his way out. Reaches for the Queen's portrait, touches it up, it falls down. He catches it, looks around, laughs, rests it on the cupboards, makes a painful exit. Silence. The CLEANER *watches him go.* MISS McKENSIE *and* MR WRIGHT *face out*)

MR WRIGHT (*his voice cracked*): 'No more ...' (*Pause*) 'No more ...' (*Pause*)

MISS McKENSIE: 'No more ...'

CLEANER: Pardon?

BOTH OF THEM (*first two lines in harmony, then disintegrating, spasmodic*)

'No more Latin, no more French,
No more sitting on the old school bench ...
No more ... spiders ... in my tea ...
Making googly ... eyes ... at me ...

(*The lights go down slowly as the* CLEANER *leans on her mop and watches them.* MR WRIGHT *has his hands between his legs, looks all around him.* MISS McKENSIE *stares out.*)

DETENTION

This play was originally commissioned by Radio WM and broadcast by them in September 1983. It was later broadcast by BBC Radio 4 in May 1984. The radio version was produced by Tim Manning and Vanessa Whitburn.

The present version has been especially revised and adapted for stage performance by the author.

Because of the many scene changes, it is not necessary to have elaborate sets, but the stage may be divided into various areas with some item of furniture to denote the scene. Scene changes may best be denoted by changes in lighting.

CHARACTERS

NICK
SARAH } teachers
JOHNSON

MRS HEPWORTH, *Headmistress*

BLOWER
MAKHAN
MANDY } pupils
TURNER
TURNER'S TWO FRIENDS

POLICE OFFICERS

ACT ONE

SCENE 1 *The school corridor.*

(*It is breaktime.* JOHNSON *is telling off* BLOWER. NICK *stands to one side.*)

JOHNSON: You're an idiot, Blower. An idiot and a perfect nuisance. What are you? (*Pause*) I said, what are you? Tell me.
BLOWER: An idiot.
JOHNSON: An idiot, what?
BLOWER: An idiot, sir.
JOHNSON: Thank you. Did you hear that, Mr Summerfield? He admitted it. He's an idiot.
NICK: Yes.
JOHNSON: At least he knows what he is. That's some hope, anyway. I don't know why I have to be bothered with the likes of you, Blower. Why should I have to waste my time standing here in the corridor, telling you off again? Can you tell me that?
BLOWER: No, sir.
JOHNSON: No. You can't. (*Pause*) I don't understand it, Mr Summerfield. He's got a lovely, modern comprehensive school here, all the facilities, everything laid on for him. But he just doesn't appreciate it, does he?
NICK: No.
JOHNSON: All he wants is to cause trouble. Well, let me tell you this, Blower. I'm sick of you causing trouble in lessons. Sick of it! Do you hear? I've just about had enough of it, and so has Mr

Summerfield. Everyone's had enough of you and your silly antics. You are not going to behave like that in one of Mr Summerfield's lessons again. Right? Now. Apologise to him. Go on.

BLOWER: Sorry, Mr Summerfield.

JOHNSON: And, just to remind you, you can have a detention for tomorrow night. Got that?

BLOWER: Yes.

JOHNSON: Yes, what?

BLOWER: Yes, sir.

JOHNSON: That's better. Now get off outside. Go on. And make sure you're at that detention tomorrow night.

(BLOWER *goes*. SARAH *has entered and stands, watching*.)

That's the only way to handle his kind. Authority. Discipline. It's the only thing they understand.

NICK: Yes. Thank you for ... sorting it out.

JOHNSON: I couldn't do much else, could I, with all that racket going on next door. I couldn't hear myself talk.

NICK: I do have trouble with Blower.

JOHNSON: We all do, Nick. But we have to learn to deal with him. We all have to learn to cope with it. It's part of our job. It's what we get paid for. You've got to learn to swim or sink. You take my advice. Learn to swim. Use a firm hand. Don't put up with any nonsense.

NICK: Yes ... I mean ... no ...

JOHNSON: Good. Well, I'd better be getting along. I've got things to do.

NICK: Thanks again ...

(JOHNSON *goes*. SARAH *approaches*.)

SARAH: Nick. What was that all about?

NICK: Oh ... nothing really ... Johnson had to come into my lesson ... I was having some trouble with Blower again.

SARAH: Oh.

NICK: I could've handled it, in my own way. He didn't have to come. Things weren't out of control. It made me look like an idiot, him coming in. How can I ever get any respect off the kids if he keeps barging in like that?

SARAH: Authority. Discipline. That's what they need. Use a firm hand. You've got to sink or swim.

NICK: That's what he said.

SARAH: I know. I've heard it before. Don't worry about it. You'll sort yourself out. Johnson always throws his weight about with new arrivals. Once you've settled down it'll get better.

NICK: He makes it sound like there's a war going on.

SARAH: Come on. Let's go to the staffroom and have a coffee. Forget about it.

NICK: Good idea. Right.

(*They go.*)

SCENE 2 *The playground.*

(BLOWER *and* MANDY *enter.*)

BLOWER: I'm gonna have him.

MANDY: Who?

BLOWER: Johnson. I'm gonna have him.

MANDY: Everybody hates him. He's horrible.

BLOWER: He can't push me around like that. I'd like to lay one on him.

MANDY: You can't do that. You'd get into real trouble then.

BLOWER: It wasn't even his lesson. It was Summerfield's.

MANDY: Soppy Summerfield?

BLOWER: Yeah. I wasn't doing anything much. Only having a bit of a laugh. Then Johnson comes marching in and starts bawling his head off. He stuck me in detention tomorrow.

MANDY: Tomorrow?

BLOWER: Yeah.

MANDY: I'm in tomorrow as well. For not doing me homework. We'll be together. We can have a laugh. (*Pause*) Kev. Are you coming to the disco tonight?

BLOWER: What disco?

MANDY: At the youth club. They've having a disco.

BLOWER: Are all the other six people going as well?

MANDY: It won't be that bad. It's something to do anyway. Better'n nothing.
BLOWER: I might.
MANDY: Go on.
BLOWER: I was going to see me grandad.
MANDY: What for?
BLOWER: He's me grandad, ain't he? He ain't very well.
MANDY: You can go and see him some other time.
BLOWER: I'll see. If Dad lets me go. He'll go mad when he hears about this detention.
MANDY: Don't tell him. I never tell my mom and dad. Are you coming then?
BLOWER: I suppose so.

(MAKHAN *enters*.)

MAKHAN: All right, Kev. Mandy.
MANDY: Right, Mak.
BLOWER: Hallo. It's the Curry Kid. Tariq the Turban.
MAKHAN: Get lost. If you ain't careful, I'll have the clan on you.
BLOWER: What clan?
MAKHAN: My clan. A secret Sikh organisation. We specialise in cutting white men's throats.
MANDY: Don't be daft.
MAKHAN: It's true. All Sikhs carry a knife with them. And if they draw it, they can't put it back until they've spilled blood.
MANDY: Where's your knife, then?
MAKHAN: I ain't got one. I don't believe in all that. It's in the blood, though. We're all warriors, right through.
BLOWER: You. You're English. You was born here. You ain't even been to India.
MANDY: You're as white as we are. Except you're brown.
MAKHAN: I wish you'd tell Turner that.
MANDY: Why? What's he been doing?
MAKHAN: You know. Same old stuff. Him and his mates standing up at the gates, chanting and clapping their hands. 'National Front, National Front.' Like a load of monkeys. Ain't got a brain between them.

Act One

MANDY: I hate Turner and his mates. They're stupid.
MAKHAN: I shut him up, though. Got him. Right on his big nose.

(*They laugh.*)

BLOWER: I wish I could've seen that.
MANDY: What did he do?
MAKHAN: Nothing. Went running off. I suppose I'll get into trouble over it now. It was worth it, though.
BLOWER: I bet it was.
MANDY: Coming to the disco tonight, Mak? Me and Kev are going.
MAKHAN: I suppose so. Yes.
BLOWER: Ain't you got to go to the temple or something?
MAKHAN: No. I told you. I don't believe in all that. Have some right arguments at home, we do. Dad wants to get me married off. I tell him to get lost. It's the same every night —

(JOHNSON *enters, off.*)

JOHNSON: Makhan!
MANDY: Look who it is.
BLOWER: What does he want?
MAKHAN: I bet I know. Turner.
JOHNSON: Makhan! Come here!
MAKHAN: I'd better go. See you.
BLOWER: See you, Mak.

(MAKHAN *goes.* JOHNSON *takes him by the arm and leads him off.*)

MANDY: He'll be in for it now.
BLOWER: I'd like to get that Turner.
MANDY: You'd like to get everybody. Come on, let's go in and sit in the library. It's cold out here.
BLOWER: They won't let us in.
MANDY: Yes, they will, if we say we're revising. Come on.
BLOWER: Right.

(*They go.*)

SCENE 3 *The staffroom.*

(NICK *and* SARAH *are sitting.*)

NICK: I wonder sometimes if I'm cut out for this job.
SARAH: Come off it, Nick. Don't start that again.
NICK: I'm just not sure.
SARAH: You've only been here a term and a half. You've got to give it a try.
NICK: Why couldn't I have got a good school for my probationary year?
SARAH: What do you mean by a good school?
NICK: One where there aren't so many problems.
SARAH: Half the problems we get we create for ourselves.
NICK: I don't know. I just don't know if I'll ever be a good teacher or not.
SARAH: And what's a good teacher? Johnson?
NICK: He gets results. We doesn't have any discipline problems. The kids respect it.
SARAH: No, they don't. They hate him. Do you want to be hated?
NICK: No, of course not. But you don't seem to have any problems either. And the kids do like you. You get on with them. You understand them.
SARAH: Don't make me your model. But you're right. You do have to try and understand their point of view. After all, we're supposed to be on their side, aren't we? They're not the enemy.
NICK: I try to. But they take advantage of me. They think I'm soft.
SARAH: It takes time, that's all. It just takes time. Don't try to rush it. As long as you believe in what you're doing, then it's all right. You've got to believe in it.
NICK: You make it sound easy.
SARAH: Well, it isn't. Look, I don't want to talk about this any more. I want to relax. I've got 3H next. I need to relax. (*Pause*) What are you doing tonight?
NICK: Tonight? Nothing.
SARAH: Fancy a meal?
NICK: A meal?

Act One

SARAH: Yes. Come round to my flat. I'll cook you a meal. I don't get much chance to show off my culinary expertise. I've got the urge to cook again.

NICK: Well ... I don't know ...

SARAH: If you don't hurry up I'll change my mind. The urge doesn't last that long.

NICK: All right, then. Yes. What time?

SARAH: About eight?

NICK: How do I get there?

SARAH: It's just up the road. Leyland Street. Number 28B.

NICK: Right. I'll be there. What are we going to have?

SARAH: Well, I can do goulash. Or there's goulash. Or I could do you some goulash.

NICK: I think I fancy goulash.

SARAH: That's a good job. It's all I can cook.

(*They laugh.* JOHNSON *enters.*)

JOHNSON: Have I missed a joke?

SARAH: No.

JOHNSON: Pity. I could do with a laugh. This seems to have been my morning for sorting out trouble. Has Nick told you about our little escapade with Blower?

SARAH: Yes. It's nothing unusual.

JOHNSON: This kind of thing seems to be on the increase, if you ask me. A general lack of discipline, I think it is. Too much soft treatment with some of them. And I've just had to deal with Makhan.

NICK: Makhan Singh?

JOHNSON: Yes. Just had him for fighting.

SARAH: That's not like him. He's a peaceful lad.

JOHNSON: Not today, he isn't. He could have broken Turner's nose.

SARAH: Turner. Well, that explains it.

JOHNSON: Does it?

SARAH: Yes. You know what Turner's like. He's always having a go at the Asians and West Indians.

JOHNSON: I see. So that makes it acceptable, does it? Because

Turner calls him a few names, it makes it all right for Makhan to hit him.

SARAH: I didn't say it. But it makes it understandable.

JOHNSON: And what if it had been the other way round, eh? What if Turner had hit Makhan? Would your reaction have been the same?

SARAH: It's not very likely that Makhan would go taunting Turner because he's white, is it?

JOHNSON: Avoiding the issue again. The old double standards. Violence is all right as long as it's on your side.

SARAH: No. I don't agree with violence. But as long as there's a race problem in this school –

JOHNSON: Don't start on that again.

SARAH: – and as long as we continue to ignore it, then this violence is going to keep on flaring up. And it's going to get worse.

JOHNSON: And what do you think about all this, Nick?

NICK: Me?

JOHNSON: Yes. What are your opinions?

NICK: Well, I'm not sure, really. I think I agree with Sarah, for the most part.

JOHNSON: Yes. I thought as much. Well, let's see how you cope with them tomorrow night, then.

NICK: What?

JOHNSON: Blower and Makhan. They're both in detention. And you're on detention duty.

NICK: Am I?

JOHNSON: Yes. Your name's on the list.

NICK: Oh. I hadn't looked at it.

JOHNSON: Always look at the lists, Nick. That's what they're there for.

(*Offstage, the school bell rings.*)

There it goes. The alarm. Battle-stations, everybody. (*Pause*) Oh, by the way, something else, Nick. Mrs Hepworth would like to have a word with you. You are free now, aren't you?

NICK: Yes.

Act One

JOHNSON: I told her you were. Back to the chalk face.

(JOHNSON *goes.*)

NICK: I wonder what she wants?
SARAH: Better go and find out. Don't worry.
NICK: No. Of course not. I won't. I'd better go.
SARAH: I'll see you later.
NICK: Yes.
SARAH: And give Mrs Hepworth my love.
NICK: What? Oh, yes. Right.

(*They both go.*)

SCENE 4   MRS HEPWORTH's *study.*

(MRS HEPWORTH *and* NICK *enter.*)

MRS HEPWORTH: Do take a seat, Mr Summerfield.
NICK: Thank you.
MRS HEPWORTH: I'm very grateful you could spare the time to come and see me. I know how precious free periods are. Especially when you're new. They give you the time to recharge the batteries.
NICK: Yes. That's right.
MRS HEPWORTH: So. How do you feel you're settling in?
NICK: Oh. All right. One or two teething problems, you know, but I am enjoying it here.
MRS HEPWORTH: I'm very pleased to hear that, Mr Summerfield. Very pleased indeed. I think it's important that staff actually enjoy their work. Find it rewarding. If we don't find it rewarding and satisfying, then we shouldn't be in the job, should we?
NICK: No. Of course not.
MRS HEPWORTH: I think I've probably told you this before, Mr Summerfield, but I think it's something worth repeating. I pride myself on having not only a lively and competent staff as far as the actual teaching goes, but also a caring staff. A compassionate staff. Those who really do care and are concerned about the

welfare of our pupils. It's what I look for in all appointments. A caring nature, a genuine concern with the great social problems and deprivations that exist in an area like this. I saw those qualities in you at your interview. That's why you were appointed here.

NICK: That's ... very kind of you to say, Mrs Hepworth ...

MRS HEPWORTH: It's the truth. I believe in speaking the truth. (*Pause*) But of course, it's not only compassion and caring that counts. We're not just social workers, are we? We're teachers.

NICK: Yes.

MRS HEPWORTH: And we have under our control some very lively youngsters. Some of them are extremely lively, I'm sure you'll agree.

NICK: Oh, yes.

MRS HEPWORTH: And they must remain under our control. If we are going to help them we must be able to control them. Set them the guidelines within which they can develop into responsible adults. They are only children still, and they need to know very much where they stand. (*Pause*) Do you take my meaning, Mr Summerfield?

NICK: Yes ...

MRS HEPWORTH: A happy school is also an efficient and a hard-working school. We mustn't forget what we demand of them, and we mustn't let them forget. After all, society is run on rules and regulations, and school is part of society, not separate from it. (*Pause*) If we let our own standards slip – if we don't maintain a form of order and reasonable discipline, how can we possibly help to alleviate the social problems that affect so many of our youngsters? We won't even be able to start. Do you agree with me, Mr Summerfield?

NICK: Yes ... of course ...

MRS HEPWORTH: Of course you do. You do have the qualities that go to make up a fine teacher, one we can be proud of here. But these qualities do take time to refine. However, I'm sure that's well within your capabilities. I'm certain that when I come to make my report on you at the end of this probationary year, I'll have no hesitation about recommending that you continue as a fully qualified Scale 1 teacher.

NICK: Thank you.

MRS HEPWORTH: Well. I won't take up any more of your precious time. Thank you for having this chat with me. I do think it's important that we all have a few minutes together, just to talk and air our views. It prevents any misunderstandings from arising, doesn't it? (*She stands.*) Well. I won't keep you, Mr Summerfield.

NICK: Right. Thank you again, Mrs Hepworth.

(NICK *goes. Pause* MRS HEPWORTH *goes.*)

SCENE 5 *The school corridor.*

(*It is after lunch.* BLOWER *enters in a hurry.* SARAH *stops him.*)

SARAH: Kevin. Kevin. Come here. (BLOWER *stops.*) Over here, Kevin. Come on.

(*He goes over to her.*)

BLOWER: Miss Steadman.
SARAH: Have you just come into school?
BLOWER: No.
SARAH: Kevin.
BLOWER: Yes, miss.
SARAH: It's a bit late, isn't it?
BLOWER: Yes, miss.
SARAH: Where've you been? I thought you stayed dinners.
BLOWER: I do.
SARAH: How come you've been out, then? Come on, Kevin. Isn't it better to tell me than to have to explain it to Mrs Hepworth?
BLOWER: I went to see my grandad, miss. He ain't very well.
SARAH: That's not a very good excuse for leaving the school premises and being late back.
BLOWER: He lives on his own. He ain't got nobody else. There's only me goes to see him. He's hurt his foot, you see, and he

can't walk very well. I had to go and clean his pigeon shed out. I promised him.

SARAH: Keeps pigeons, does he?

BLOWER: Yes, miss. He used to have the best round here. They won all the races.

SARAH: Doesn't he race them now?

BLOWER: No. He's too old. And he ain't got many left.

SARAH: That sounds interesting. I'd like to come round and see them sometime, if your grandad wouldn't mind.

BLOWER: Do you like pigeons, then?

SARAH: My father used to keep them.

BLOWER: Your dad? He didn't did he?

SARAH: Yes, he did. Look, I'd love to talk to you about pigeons, but I think it'll have to be some other time. You'd better get off to your lesson, quick. You're late enough as it is. And see that next time you have to go out you get permission first. All right?

BLOWER: Yes, miss.

(*He starts to go.* JOHNSON *enters.*)

JOHNSON: What are you doing out of lessons, Blower? (BLOWER *stops.*) Did you hear me? I asked you a question. What are you doing out of lessons?

BLOWER: I'm just going.

JOHNSON: I can see that. I want to know why you aren't there now.

SARAH: It's all right, Mr Johnson, I've just sorted everything out.

JOHNSON: I'd like to hear what he's got to say for himself.

BLOWER: I just told Miss Steadman.

JOHNSON: Tell me, then.

BLOWER: I had to go and see my grandad. He ain't well and –

JOHNSON: And you've only just got back into school.

BLOWER: Yes.

JOHNSON: Did you get permission to go and see your poor sick grandad?

BLOWER: No.

JOHNSON: Then you shouldn't have gone, then, should you?

Act One

BLOWER: No.
JOHNSON: No, sir!
BLOWER: No, sir!
SARAH: I have been through all this with him, Mr Johnson. I've told him he's not to do it again.
JOHNSON: Just telling's not enough for this one, Miss Steadman. It doesn't go in. There seems to be a blockage in there somewhere. A blockage between one ear and the other. What it needs is knocking out, isn't it, Blower?
BLOWER: Just you try it.
JOHNSON: Don't speak to me like that.
SARAH: Kevin –
BLOWER: Try touching me and see what you get –

(JOHNSON *slaps him. Pause.*)

JOHNSON: That's quite enough of that. Well, Blower, what am I going to get. Mm? (*Pause*) Get along to your lesson now. And be thankful I don't take this any further. (BLOWER *goes. Pause*) Only thing his kind understand, Sarah. Violence. It's their language. You have to learn to speak it sometimes. That way you stand a chance of getting through to them.
SARAH: There was no need for it.
JOHNSON: You heard the cheek he was giving me. He made a threat.
SARAH: I mean there was no need for any of it. No need for you to even interfere. It had all been sorted out.
JOHNSON: You can't let someone like Blower get away with a soft option. He'll just try it on all the more next time.
SARAH: You undermined my authority. I am a teacher in this school, you know. You're not the only one.
JOHNSON: I was simply doing my job, Sarah. I am responsible for Upper School welfare, you know.
SARAH: You interfere. You think no one's capable of dealing with any problem except you.
JOHNSON: I was simply backing you up –
SARAH: Backing me up! Listen to me, Mr Johnson. I don't want you to undermine my authority again. Right?

JOHNSON: I wish you'd lower your voice in the corridor, Sarah.
SARAH: You won't do it again! Right!
JOHNSON: I wasn't undermining your authority. And in any case, this is hardly the time and the place for a discussion like this.
SARAH: If you do it again, I shall go straight to the union and report you for hitting Kevin Blower. Do you understand? (JOHNSON *does not answer*) Good. Now. I've got a lesson to go to.

(SARAH *goes.* JOHNSON *stares after her. He goes.*)

SCENE 6 *That night, outside the youth club.*

(MANDY *and* MAKHAN *are waiting for* BLOWER.)

MANDY: He should be here by now.
MAKHAN: He'll be along.
MANDY: It's half past eight.
MAKHAN: That's early yet.
MANDY: I'm getting bored standing out here.
MAKHAN: Go inside, then. I'll wait for him.
MANDY: No. I said I'd wait. (*Pause*) Did you hear what Johnson did to him today?
MAKHAN: No.
MANDY: Hit him. Slapped him round the head.
MAKHAN: Hit Kev?
MANDY: Yeah. It shouldn't be allowed.
MAKHAN: That ain't allowed.
MANDY: You try telling somebody about Johnson. Who'd listen to us?
MAKHAN: Could give it a try. Mrs Hepworth's always going on about how we should start acting like responsible citizens, how we should think about our rights and all the rest of it. Well, let's start.
MANDY: How'd you mean?
MAKHAN: We all know teachers ain't allowed to smack kids. Only the Head or the Deputy Head can give corporal

punishment. So. Let's go and complain. To Mrs Hepworth. Report Johnson.
MANDY: I'd like to see you try.
MAKHAN: I will. If Kev'll come with me.
MANDY: It'll be Kev's word against Johnson's. I know who they'll believe.
MAKHAN: We've got to start somewhere. We can't let somebody like Johnson just keep pushing us around. We've got to fight back sometime. Do something.
MANDY: That's what Kev was saying. He was saying today how the next time Johnson did something to him, he was gonna let him have it. Said he didn't care what happened.
MAKHAN: That's stupid, and Kev knows it is. You don't get anywhere doing things like that. Just get called a thug or a hooligan and get suspended from school. You got to do things their way. Make them listen to you.
MANDY: That won't ever happen.
MAKHAN: It might, if we try ... we've got to try ...

(TURNER *and his two mates enter.*)

TURNER: Look what we got here, then.
MANDY: Blimey. Somebody must've left the top off their dustbin. Something's crawled out.
FIRST MATE: It's Sambo.
SECOND MATE: Woghead.
TURNER: What you doing here?
MAKHAN: Mind your own business, Turner.
TURNER: It is my business, wog.
FIRST MATE: Yeah. That's right. It's our business.
SECOND MATE: So tell us. Come on.
MANDY: Get lost, Turner.
TURNER: And what you doing with him? Does Kev know about this?
FIRST MATE: We'll tell him.
MANDY: Just get lost.
TURNER: No. We ain't gonna get lost. He is. Go on.
MAKHAN: I ain't moving.

SECOND MATE: He's acting brave.
FIRST MATE: Pretending he's the big hero.
MAKHAN: Course, you two was really brave this morning, wasn't you? So brave you ran all the way in to tell Johnson what had happened. By the way, Turner. How's your nose?
MANDY: Looks a bit flatter than the last time I seen it.
TURNER: Shurrup.
FIRST MATE: Or we'll shut you up.
MANDY: I'm so scared. I dunno what I'm gonna do.
TURNER: I know what I'm gonna do. I'm gonna give this wog just ten seconds to get away from here, and if he ain't gone by then, he's gonna get smashed into the ground.
MANDY: Why should he go, Turner?
TURNER: 'Cos this place ain't for his kind. It's for whites only.
MANDY: There ain't no sign saying that.
SECOND MATE: There should be.
MANDY: You lot wouldn't be able to read it if there was.
TURNER: Come on. Are you going? Eh? Why don't you go back to your own country?
FIRST MATE: Yeah. Go back to curry country.
TURNER: 'Cos if you don't, do you know what's gonna happen? To you and all your kind?
MAKHAN: No. Tell me.
TURNER: We're gonna stick you all in the gas-chambers.
MANDY: You're disgusting, Turner.
TURNER: And anybody who's friends with them. They're all gonna go into the gas-chambers.
SECOND MATE: Starting with you.
TURNER: Right. Get him.

(TURNER *and his mates attack* MAKHAN.)

MANDY: No. Stop it! Gerroff him!

(MANDY *grabs one of the mates by the hair. She hits him.* BLOWER *enters.*

Kev! Quick! Help!

(*He runs on and grabs* TURNER.)

Act One

BLOWER: Get off him, Turner. If you want to have a go with somebody, have a go with me.
TURNER: Right.

(*They start to fight.*)

FIRST MATE: The coppers! Come on.

(TURNER *breaks free.*)

TURNER: I'll have you, Blower.

(TURNER *and his mates run.*)

BLOWER: You all right, Mak?
MAKHAN: Yeah. They didn't do any damage.
MANDY: Here come the coppers.

(*Two* POLICE OFFICERS *approach.*)

FIRST OFFICER: All right, you lot, what's going on?
BLOWER: Nothing.
FIRST OFFICER: It didn't look like nothing. Who were that lot running away?
BLOWER: I dunno.
SECOND OFFICER: Never seen them before, I suppose.
BLOWER: That's right.
FIRST OFFICER: What was going on, then?
MANDY: They set on him.
FIRST OFFICER: Set on who?
MANDY: Him. Mak.
BLOWER: I was just breaking it up.
SECOND OFFICER: Tell us what happened.
BLOWER: I just said –
SECOND OFFICER: I'm not talking to you. I'm talking to him. What happened?
MAKHAN: We were just standing here and they came across and set on me.
SECOND OFFICER: Just standing minding your own business, were you?
MAKHAN: That's right. We were waiting to go into the disco.

FIRST OFFICER: And they started beating you up for no reason?
MANDY: It was 'cos he's black.
FIRST OFFICER: Is that right? How do you know?
MAKHAN: They said.
SECOND OFFICER: This was a racial attack, then, was it?
BLOWER: Don't you think you should be chasing after them instead of standing here talking to us? They're the ones that caused all the trouble —
FIRST OFFICER: We don't need you to tell us our business, sonny. Just keep out of this.
SECOND OFFICER: You're calling this a racial attack?
MAKHAN: I suppose so.
MANDY: That's what it was, yeah.
SECOND OFFICER: Are you hurt?
MAKHAN: Not much.
BLOWER: He would've been if I hadn't got here.
FIRST OFFICER: I've told you.
SECOND OFFICER: Do you want to come down to the station with us?
MAKHAN: What for?
SECOND OFFICER: To make a statement.
FIRST OFFICER: If you've got a complaint, come and make a statement. Give us all the details. (*Pause*) Well?
MAKHAN: No. I don't want to make no statement.
SECOND OFFICER: Sure?
MAKHAN: Yes.
FIRST OFFICER: All right, then. You'd better get along off home. The three of you.
MANDY: We're going into the disco.
FIRST OFFICER: I think you'd be better going home. You don't want anymore trouble, do you?
MANDY: There won't be any more trouble.
SECOND OFFICER: That youth club's nothing but trouble. There's hardly a night goes by when something doesn't happen. It seems that kids these days can't enjoy themselves without getting into a fight or smashing something up.
BLOWER: We haven't caused any trouble.

Act One

FIRST OFFICER: You will be soon if you don't stop interrupting us.
MAKHAN: Come on, Kev. Let's go. I don't feel like goking in now anyway.
SECOND OFFICER: That's sensible.
MANDY: I wanted to go to the disco.
BLOWER: We'll go another night. Come on.

(BLOWER, MANDY *and* MAKHAN *go*.)

FIRST OFFICER: I dunno. This area. There's always something, isn't there? Sometimes I think the best thing that could do would be to pull it all down and start again.
SECOND OFFICER: There'd still be trouble.
FIRST OFFICER: I suppose you're right.

(*They go.*)

SCENE 7   SARAH's *flat*.

(SARAH *and* NICK *enter*.)

SARAH: I made a fool of myself. I shouldn't have let him get to me like that.
NICK: Who?
SARAH: Johnson. This afternoon. That thing with Kevin Blower.
NICK: Oh. Yes.
SARAH: I lost my temper. I got out of control. He loved that. I could see by his face. He was so superior.
NICK: He's always like that with me. I'm scared of him. I sometimes wonder who I am more scared of. Him, or the kids.
SARAH: You're not scared of the kids?
NICK: Some of them. I don't mind admitting it. Aren't you?
SARAH: No.
NICK: I am. Blower, for instance. I don't know what I'd do if he really started playing up. I don't know how I'd handle him.
SARAH: Blower's all right, really. He's not bad. He's got a lot of frustrations inside him. The thing is to try and understand that, and to let him see that you're trying. That you're on his side.

NICK: I don't know. I get sick in the mornings, sometimes. Worrying. About whether I'll get through the day without any trouble. Whether I'll pass my probationary year. Whether I'm even good enough.

SARAH: Perhaps you worry too much about yourself. There are nine hundred kids who need worrying about as well.

NICK: I can't help it. I feel like I'm lost, floundering. I don't have any kind of discipline.

SARAH: That's not the most important thing.

NICK: But there's got to be some sort of discipline.

SARAH: You mean like slapping kids round the head? Like Johnson did to Blower?

NICK: No . . .

SARAH: That's not what teaching's about. That's got nothing to do with teaching. It's just force. Power. A bigger boy bullying a smaller boy. I came into teaching to try and do something. To improve things, make things better. School's the one place that can do that, change society for the better. But the institution – all its petty rules and regulations – I sometimes think it's changing me –

NICK: Do you know why I came into teaching?

SARAH: No. Tell me.

NICK: Because my parents wanted me to. Right from when I was little, they used to say to me: 'Be a teacher, Nick.' It was a step up the ladder for them. I was the bright boy of the family. Working-class child makes good. I never even questioned it, never thought about it. Until one morning I woke up, and I was a teacher. And it scared me. I never even made a choice. (*Pause*) You see? I don't have your conviction, Sarah.

SARAH: You've got more conviction than Johnson.

NICK: No. You're wrong. Johnson believes in his way. He believes he's right, that he knows how it should be done. And who knows? Maybe he is right.

SARAH: You can't say that.

NICK: Are you sure he's not right?

SARAH: Yes.

(Pause.)

NICK: I'd better be going. It's getting late. I've still got some worrying to do.
SARAH: What now?
NICK: This detention I've got to take tomorrow.
SARAH: That'll be all right.
NICK: Blower's there.
SARAH: Listen. I'm not doing anything after school tomorrow. I'll come in with you.
NICK: You don't have to.
SARAH: I know I don't. We can share it. It'll make the time pass more quickly.
NICK: All right. If you're sure you don't mind ...
SARAH: I don't. *(Pause)* Do you have to go?
NICK: Yes. I have got some work to do.
SARAH: Duty calls. All right.
NICK: Thanks for the meal. It was lovely.
SARAH: You'll have to come over again.
NICK: I will. *(Pause)* Well, then. I'll be off.
SARAH: Listen.

(Pause.)

NICK: What?
SARAH: Can't you hear it? That noise, outside.
NICK: It's just some kids shouting.
SARAH: Just some kids. Our kids. The ones we teach. They're out there, in the dark somewhere. Not far away. But what do we know about them? What do we know about their lives? *(Pause)* You hear them? Shouting? They're the ones we should be listening to.

(They stand and listen as the noise of kids shouting rises. Lights to blackout.)

ACT TWO

SCENE 1 *A classroom.*

(BLOWER, MAKHAN *and* MANDY *are present.*)

MANDY: There ain't nobody here. Only us.
BLOWER: Don't seem worth staying, does it?
MAKHAN: Anybody know who's on?
BLOWER: No.
MANDY: It might be Johnson.
MAKHAN: That'd be just our luck.
BLOWER: Come on. Let's go.
MANDY: We can't. We might get seen going down the corridor.
BLOWER: Out the window, then.
MANDY: What?

(BLOWER *goes to a window at the back and raises it.*)

BLOWER: Climb out the window.
MANDY: Don't be daft.

(MAKHAN *looks out of the window.*)

MAKHAN: You'd have to jump.
BLOWER: It ain't very far. Only one floor up. Do it easy.
MANDY: I ain't gonna jump out the window.
BLOWER: You ain't got no sense of adventure.
MAKHAN: Hey, Kev. Did you bring that knife in?
BLOWER: Oh, yeah. Here it is. (*He takes out a knife.*) It's a beauty, ain't it?

Act Two

MAKHAN: Not bad.
BLOWER: Beat one of your Sikh knives any day.
MANDY: What you brought that in for, Kev? You'll get had if somebody sees you with that.
BLOWER: I only brought it in to show Mak. It's me grandad's. He's had it since he was a kid. He used to kill rats with it.
MANDY: No, he didn't.
BLOWER: He did. Used to kill them and cut off their tails, he told me.
MAKHAN: What for?
BLOWER: Sell them.
MAKHAN: Who'd want to buy rats' tails?
BLOWER: I dunno. That's what he used it for, though. And other things as well.
MANDY: Like what?
BLOWER: Skinning rabbits. There used to be a farm round here. Rose's farm. Grandad used to go poaching rabbits off it. He got caught once, and –

(*The door opens.* NICK *enters.* BLOWER *quickly puts the knife away.*)

NICK: Right, everybody. Sit down. (*They stare at him.*) Come on. Sit down.
MANDY: Are you on detention with us, sir?
NICK: Yes, that's right, Mandy. Now sit down, please.
BLOWER: I said we should've jumped out the window.

(*They sit.*)

NICK: Is this everyone? Just you three?
MANDY: Looks like it, sir.
BLOWER: Look in your register.
NICK: What's that, Blower?
BLOWER: The detention register, sir. All the names should be in there.
NICK: Should they? Oh. I see.
MAKHAN: Haven't you got it with you, sir?

NICK: No ... no one told me about a register ... well, never mind.
MANDY: I think there should be some others here, sir.
NICK: Yes.
BLOWER: But as you ain't got the register ...
NICK: All right, Blower. That's enough. You three will have to do. I presume you've all been given some work to do?
MAKHAN: Yes.
NICK: Right, then. You'd better get on with it. And quietly, please. No talking. This is supposed to be a detention.

(*Pause. The three make half-hearted attempts to start work.* NICK *sits at the desk.*
   MANDY *takes a transistor radio out of her bag and switches it on.*)

What's that?
MANDY: It's a radio, sir.
NICK: Yes, Mandy. I can see that. What's it doing here?
MANDY: I'm listening to it.
NICK: Switch it off, please.
MANDY: Oh, sir. I always listen to the radio when I'm working. It helps me to concentrate.
NICK: There are others who might not be able to.
BLOWER: I don't mind. Do you, Mak?
MAKHAN: No.
NICK: I do. I have work to do as well.
MANDY: Go on, Mr Summerfield.
NICK: No. Now please switch that radio off.
MANDY: All right.

(*She turns the radio off.*)

NICK: Now please get on with your work.

(*They work quietly for a time.*)

MANDY: Sir.
NICK: Yes, Mandy?
MANDY: If we finish our work early, can we go?

Act Two

NICK: You're supposed to be here for an hour.
MANDY: Yeah, but if I finish before that, there ain't no point in just sitting around doing nothing, is there?
NICK: That's all part of the punishment.
BLOWER: I think that's daft.
NICK: It doesn't matter what you think, Kevin.
MAKHAN: We know that.
NICK: Pardon, Makhan? What did you say?
MAKHAN: It never matters what we think, does it?
NICK: I wouldn't say that.
MAKHAN: I would.
MANDY: We always go when we've finished.
NICK: No, you don't. You stay till detention's finished.
BLOWER: I'm supposed to do a paper round. If I go early I can still get it done.
NICK: You should've thought of that yesterday, shouldn't you?
MAKHAN: He sounds like Johnson. They all end up sounding the same.
NICK: Get on with your work, Makhan.
MAKHAN: See?
NICK: Makhan. That's enough! Now get on with the work you've got. I don't particularly like being here, you know. It's no fun for me either.
BLOWER: So you'll let us go when we've finished then, sir? We won't tell if you don't.
MANDY: Go on, sir. It's all daft anyway.
NICK: None of you have even started your work yet. It's about time you did –

(SARAH *enters*.)

SARAH: Hallo. Sorry I'm a bit late.
NICK: That's all right.
SARAH: Is this all there is?
NICK: It seems like it.
SARAH: Who's on the register?
BLOWER: He ain't got it, miss.

NICK: Blower! (*To* SARAH) I didn't know anything about a register. No one told me you have to have one.
SARAH: That's typical of this place, isn't it? Never mind. It makes it easier for us, doesn't it?
BLOWER: Reckon he fancies her?
MANDY: I dunno.
BLOWER: I think he does. He's gone red, look.
NICK: Quiet, please.
MANDY: Miss Steadman.
SARAH: Yes, Mandy?
MANDY: Does Mr Summerfield fancy you?

(*Laughter.*)

SARAH: I don't think that's really any of your business, is it?
MANDY: Kevin thinks he does.
NICK: That's quite enough now. I think you'd better get on with your work, or you'll never get it finished.
MAKHAN: It's boring. Look what they've given us to do. A real waste of time.
NICK: That's not my fault. Just get on with it.

(*Pause.*)

SARAH: Oh, Makhan. I've got a warning for you. Apparently, I've heard that your friend Turner is after your blood.
MAKHAN: Tell me something new.
SARAH: He's hanging around waiting for you. I should be careful when you go home.
MAKHAN: Thanks, miss.
NICK: What's all this about?
SARAH: There was some trouble last night, at the youth club. Isn't that right?
MAKHAN: That's right.
MANDY: Me and Mak was waiting for Kev when Turner and two of his mates come up and started in on Mak. Kev come along and broke it up.
BLOWER: That Turner's gonna get what's coming to him one of these days.

MANDY: Why don't the school do anything about him, miss? He's always causing trouble, but nothing ever happens to him. We get into trouble, but he's worse than us.
BLOWER: He's evil.
MANDY: Like yesterday. Mak only hit him 'cos he was going on about his colour. You can't blame Mak. I'd do the same. But Johnson put Mak in detention and left Turner alone.
MAKHAN: Johnson's just an idiot.
NICK: That's enough of that, Makhan. Mr Johnson is —
BLOWER: A pain in the —
NICK: Blower!
SARAH: All right, Kevin. No more.
MANDY: Why don't the school do anything, though?
SARAH: Because Turner's clever. He never lets himself get caught. Not like you lot.
NICK: If Turner is hanging around, don't you think we ought to do something about it?
SARAH: There's not much we can do at the moment. I'll see Mrs Hepworth about it tomorrow. I meant to see her today, but I didn't get the time. She's been interviewing all day.
BLOWER: A lot she'll do anyway.
NICK: Quiet! (*Pause*) Roll on a quarter to five. I don't know who it was that invented detention, but it wasn't a teacher.
SARAH: Why's that?
NICK: It's just as much a punishment for us as for them, isn't it?
SARAH: Yes. I suppose it is. (*Pause*) Had a good day today?
NICK: Not bad, actually. One of the better ones.
SARAH: Good. You see? I told you things weren't that bad.
NICK: Don't speak too soon. The day's not over yet.
SARAH: Nothing's going to happen here, is it? We'll go for a cup of tea in town, afterwards, if you like. There's a new French café opened. Mock-French, anyway. But it beats a McDonalds.
NICK: Anything beats a McDonalds.
MANDY: Mr Summerfield.
NICK: Now what, Mandy?
MANDY: I think there's somebody at the door.
NICK: What?

MANDY: I think I can see somebody, just outside.
NICK: Who can that be? I'd better have a look. (*He crosses to the door, opens it, sees* TURNER *there.*) Turner. What are you doing here?
TURNER: I'm waiting.
NICK: What for?
TURNER: Him. In there.
NICK: Get away from here, Turner. You shouldn't be here. Go on.

(SARAH *crosses.*)

SARAH: What do you want?
TURNER: I'm waiting for that wog.
SARAH: Get out of here, Turner.
TURNER: No.
NICK: Turner. Did you hear what we said?
TURNER: I ain't going till I've seen him.
SARAH: If you don't go now, Turner, I'll have you reported tomorrow.

(TURNER *does not move.*)

NICK: Come on. Off you go.

(*He goes to place his hand on* TURNER's *arm.* TURNER *pushes him away.*)

TURNER: Don't you touch me.
SARAH: Turner.
NICK: Don't you dare –

(*He grabs at* TURNER. TURNER *hits him and pushes his way into the room.*)

TURNER: Right, wog. I'm gonna get you.

(*He grabs at* MAKHAN.)

SARAH: Turner! Stop it!
BLOWER: I been waiting for them, Turner.

(*He grabs* TURNER. *They start to fight.*)

NICK: Stop it! All of you! Just stop it!

(*They ignore him and fight across the room.*)

Can't we do anything?

SARAH: Stop this!

(*She tries to part* TURNER *and* BLOWER *but gets pushed out of the way. She cries out.*)

NICK: Are you all right?
SARAH: Yes.
NICK: Makhan. Mandy. Can't you stop them?
MANDY: No.
MAKHAN: It's Turner. He's the one.

(TURNER *suddenly cries out.* BLOWER *stands back from him. He has his knife in his hand.* TURNER *staggers against a desk. Pause.*)

NICK: My God. What have you done?
MANDY: Kev!
BLOWER: He asked for it.
MAKHAN: You stabbed him.
BLOWER: He had it coming to him.
SARAH: Is he all right?

(NICK *takes hold of* TURNER, *examines him.*)

NICK: It doesn't look very bad. Just a flesh wound, I think. (*He lies* TURNER *down.*) He needs help, though. (*He turns to* BLOWER.) You idiot, Blower. What are you doing with that knife anyway? Give it to me.
BLOWER: No.
NICK: What? Did you hear me? I said give me the knife.
BLOWER: No.
NICK: Come on, Blower. Don't be more stupid than you have been already. You're in enough trouble as it is. Now give me the knife.
BLOWER: You ain't having it.
NICK: Don't be so thick!
BLOWER: Keep back!

(*He threatens* NICK *with the knife.*)

SARAH: Kevin. What are you doing?
BLOWER: You keep back as well.
MANDY: Give him the knife, Kev.
BLOWER: Nobody's taking this knife off me. You know what'll happen. Soon as I give it up they'll call the coppers, and then we'll all be in it. Not just me. You and all.
SARAH: You're making it worse.
BLOWER: It can't get much worse, can it?
NICK: For pity's sake, will you see some sense, Blower, and stop acting so stupid –
BLOWER: And will you stop calling me stupid! I'm sick of being called stupid. I ain't stupid! All right? So stop calling me stupid. You're the one who's stupid. You can't see that if you come any nearer to me you're gonna get this in the gut! (*Pause*) I'm in control now. (*Pause*) You all right, Mak?
MAKHAN: Yeah. What are we gonna do now?
BLOWER: I dunno. All I know is I ain't giving this knife up and I ain't letting them two go. I'm in control.
NICK: Make him see some sense, Makhan.
BLOWER: Shut up, Summerfield.
SARAH: Think what you're doing, Kevin.
BLOWER: I'm trying to think, only you won't let me. You keep talking. Haven't you talked enough for one day? Ain't it about time you give it a rest? I'm sick of being talked at and pushed around all the time by you lot. I'm gonna do some of the pushing now.
MANDY: What's gonna happen, Kev?
BLOWER: I don't know yet. I'll think of something.
SARAH: What about Turner?
BLOWER: What about him?
SARAH: He's bleeding.
BLOWER: Let him bleed.
SARAH: He needs to go to hospital.
MAKHAN: We don't want Turner hanging around here, Kev. It'll be best to get him to hospital.

BLOWER: How?
MAKHAN: One of us can go down and phone.

(*Pause.*)

BLOWER: Yeah. And then the coppers come.
MAKHAN: But they won't do anything while we got these two, will they?
BLOWER: What do you mean?
MAKHAN: We've got hostages.
BLOWER: Hostages. Yeah! Like a siege. Like on the telly. They won't be able to do anything.
NICK: Listen to him. He thinks he's a terrorist now. He doesn't know what he's talking about.
BLOWER: Right. I've warned you enough. You've asked for it now.

(*He moves towards* NICK. MAKHAN *stops him.*)

MAKHAN: No, Kev. We don't want to hurt anybody. We want people to listen to us.
SARAH: What do you mean?
MAKHAN: People'll have to listen to us, now, miss, won't they? They can't just drag us away and ignore us. While we've got you here, they'll have to listen to what we've got to say. Our side of things.
BLOWER: Hey! The newspapers might come. Even the telly. We'll be famous.
MANDY: I don't want to be famous.
BLOWER: Shut up, Mandy. You're in this with us as well. Right?
MANDY: Don't talk to me like that.
BLOWER: I'm just telling you –
MANDY: You don't tell me nothing. You never talk to me like that. Nobody does.
BLOWER: All right. But you're with us, ain't you?
MANDY: Say you're sorry.
BLOWER: What?
MANDY: Say you're sorry for talking to me like that first. Go on.

(*Pause.*)

BLOWER: I'm sorry.
MANDY: Right.

(TURNER *moans.*)

SARAH: I think you'd better do something about Turner.
MAKHAN: Yeah. Who's gonna go and phone?
MANDY: I will.
MAKHAN: Go on, then. Don't be long.
MANDY: I won't.

(MANDY *goes out.*)

NICK: I can't believe this is happening.
BLOWER: You better. 'Cos it is.
MAKHAN: Miss Steadman, Mr Summerfield. Sit down over there. By the desk. (*They do so*) That's right. Now, you stay there. Don't move, whatever happens. You know we don't want to hurt you.
BLOWER: But if you do try anything, just remember I've got this knife. (*Pause*) Do you want to know about this knife? Shall I tell you about it? It's my grandad's. He got it from his dad, and he got it in the First World War, off a German soldier. You wouldn't think it was that old, would you? He's always kept it looking good, sharpened it, oiled it. It's a good knife, ain't it?

(*He is pushing the knife close to* NICK's *face.*)

NICK: Keep it away from my face.
BLOWER: It's a good knife!
NICK: All right! It's a good knife.
MAKHAN: Kev.
BLOWER: What?
MAKHAN: Leave it.
BLOWER: I'm just showing him my knife.
MAKHAN: Just leave it, Kev. We don't want any of that.

(TURNER *groans.*)

Act Two

SARAH: How is he?

(MAKHAN *looks at him.*)

MAKHAN: I don't know.
TURNER: I'm cold.
BLOWER: He's cold.
MAKHAN: Let's have a look at you.

(*He moves* TURNER.)

TURNER: Get your hands off me.
MAKHAN: There ain't much you can do about it now, is there?
TURNER: I'm dying.
BLOWER: You ain't dying, Turner.
TURNER: When I'm better, I'm gonna get you.
BLOWER: You don't give up, do you?
NICK: Makhan, why don't you stop this, now, before it's too late.
MAKHAN: I think it's already too late.
NICK: You're intelligent. You can make something of yourself. You've got a future.
MAKHAN: Have I?
NICK: Yes. But you won't have if you carry on with this.
BLOWER: Don't listen to him, Mak. He's just trying to get you to give up. Trying to turn us against each other. That's right, ain't it, Summerfield?
SARAH: He's right, Kevin, you know he is. This isn't going to get you anywhere.
BLOWER: Yes it is. It's gonna get our names in the papers. It's gonna give us some power for once. It's gonna make people listen to us for once.
NICK: And what are you going to tell them?

(*Pause.* MANDY *enters.*)

MAKHAN: Have you phoned?
MANDY: Yes. But Johnson saw me, while I was in the entrance hall. He shouted after me.
MAKHAN: What did you do?
MANDY: I ran up here. I think he's coming up after me.

BLOWER: What's Johnson doing here? He always goes home straight after school.
MAKHAN: He didn't tonight. Let's get this desk in front of the door, quick, so he can't get in.

(MANDY *and* MAKHAN *drag a desk and jam it in front of the door.*)

BLOWER (*to* NICK *and* SARAH): Right, you two. Make sure you stay where you are. Don't move. And let us do the talking to Johnson.
MANDY: Kev. I'm scared.
BLOWER: What of?
MANDY: This. What we're doing. It don't seem right. I don't even know how we got into it.
BLOWER: We're in it now, and we're all in it together. Nothing can happen to us, not as long as we've got these two. We're on top. We've got to keep it like that.
SARAH: For how long, though?
BLOWER: As long as we like.
SARAH: You can't stay here forever. You're going to have to go out sometime.
MAKHAN: We'll decide when that is. And it'll be on our terms.
BLOWER: We'll make demands.
MAKHAN: Safe passage.
BLOWER: A million quid in a suitcase.
MAKHAN: An aeroplane to South America.
BLOWER: Anything we want.
NICK: You think it's a game. Just a game. Like a film you've seen on television. It's not real, is it?
BLOWER: Oh, yeah. It's real enough. This knife says so.

(JOHNSON *appears outside the door.*)

JOHNSON: What's going on in there? Mr Summerfield?
MAKHAN: Get against the desk. Make sure he can't get in.
JOHNSON: Makhan. I can see you. What are you doing there?
MAKHAN: What are you doing there?
JOHNSON: Open this door at once.
BLOWER: Get lost, Johnson.

Act Two

JOHNSON: Mr Summerfield. Are you in there?
NICK: Yes.
JOHNSON: Will you kindly explain to me what is going on?
NICK: It's Blower and –
BLOWER: Shut up! I said we'd do the talking.
MAKHAN: Listen to me, Johnson, and don't interrupt.
JOHNSON: How dare you talk –
MAKHAN: I said don't interrupt. Just listen, for once in your life. There's been an accident in here. Turner's got himself hurt –
JOHNSON: Turner?
MAKHAN: Listen! He's hurt, and we've phoned for an ambulance. We'll put him out in the corridor after you've gone so they can get him. It was his own fault he got hurt. He came looking for trouble and he got it.
JOHNSON: I don't understand what you're talking –
MAKHAN: If you'd listen, you might. We ain't coming out. Not yet. We've got Mr Summerfield and Miss Steadman here, and we're holding them hostage with a knife –
JOHNSON: What –
MAKHAN: A knife. We're holding them.
JOHNSON: Let me in here.

(*He pushes against the door.* MAKHAN *and* MANDY *push against the desk.*)

Will you let me in?
MAKHAN: No. We won't.
BLOWER: If you try to come in, there'll be somebody else hurt, and it'll be your fault.

(JOHNSON *stops pushing.*)

JOHNSON: I've never heard anything so ridiculous in my life –
BLOWER: Shut your trap, Johnson. We ain't interested in what you've heard.
MAKHAN: We're holding them. This is a siege.
JOHNSON: Do you want me to call Mrs Hepworth? Do you want me to call the police?
BLOWER: Yeah. You call them. And the newspapers. And the

telly. Get them all out here. But we ain't coming out till we're ready. We ain't coming out till you meet our terms.
JOHNSON: You've got terms, have you? And what are they?
MAKHAN: We'll let you know.
JOHNSON: You won't dare use that knife.
BLOWER: Want a bet? I've already used it once on Turner.
MAKHAN: There's the three of us in here. Me, Kev and Mandy. You tell them how it is. You tell them what's happening.
BLOWER: Yeah. Go on. Run along now, Johnson. Be a good boy.
JOHNSON: I'm going. I'm going to phone Mrs Hepworth right away, and then I'm going to call the police. We'll have this stupid little escapade of yours stopped in no time, and then you'll all be for it. I only hope for your sakes they don't let me get my hands on you first! Miss Steadman? Mr Summerfield? I'll be back. Don't you worry.

(*He goes. Pause.*)

MAKHAN: He's gone.

(MAKHAN, MANDY *and* BLOWER *burst into laughter.*)

BLOWER: Did you see him? Did you see his face?
MANDY: Went all red. I thought he was going to burst.
MAKHAN: And he was spitting all down his chin.
BLOWER: He didn't know what to do. Johnson didn't know what to do.
MANDY: He was stuck.
MAKHAN: We pulled one over on Johnson. It's been worth it just for that.
MANDY: I bet he'll never be the same again.

(*They laugh.*)

SARAH: Don't you think you'd better get Turner outside?
BLOWER: All right. We was just going to. Mak, take him out.
MAKHAN: Right. (*He picks up* TURNER *and carries him out of the door*)
TURNER: I'm gonna get you for this.
MAKHAN: Yeah. Course you are.

Act Two

NICK: Why don't you stop all this now? You've had your fun. Miss Steadman and I will both speak up for you. We'll say it wasn't your fault.
SARAH: We understand you. Really.
MANDY: You understand us, do you?
SARAH: Yes!
BLOWER: Don't give us that. Anyway, it's too late now. Johnson'll be out to get us whatever you two say.

(MAKHAN *comes back in. He drags the desk back in front of the door.*)

MAKHAN: Right. That's it. We're in business now.
NICK: I wish you'd think twice about what you were doing.
BLOWER: There ain't nothing to think about any more.

(MANDY *looks out of the window. Ambulance siren, off.*)

MANDY: The ambulance is here.
MAKHAN: Yeah. And the coppers won't be far behind.
MANDY: This is really happening, ain't it?
BLOWER: That's right.
MANDY: It's really happening.

(*Fade lights.*)

SCENE 2 *Outside, in the playground.*

(MRS HEPWORTH *and* JOHNSON *together.*)

MRS HEPWORTH: I don't understand it. It's beyond me. We try out best to help these children. We know the circumstances they live in, we do our best to make allowances for it – to be understanding and sympathetic. But it doesn't seem to be enough for them, does it?
JOHNSON: Well, if you don't mind my saying so, Mrs Hepworth, I think we've been a bit too soft with them.
MRS HEPWORTH: Yes. I do know your views.
JOHNSON: I could have predicted something like this would happen some day.

MRS HEPWORTH: Could you?

(*Pause.*)

JOHNSON: What are the police doing? I wish they'd get on and do something.

MRS HEPWORTH: I'm sure they're doing everything that's necessary. It's best if we leave it in their hands now. (*Pause*) I only wish I knew what it was they wanted.

JOHNSON: They said they had some terms. The cheek of it! I'd give them terms if I caught hold of them.

MRS HEPWORTH: Why don't they tell us what they are?

JOHNSON: Because they haven't got any really. It's just talk. Empty talk from empty heads. They've got themselves into a situation and they don't know what to do with it. So they just say the first stupid thing that comes into their heads. If it wasn't so serious it would be laughable. A right farce.

MRS HEPWORTH: It's Mr Summerfield and Miss Steadman I feel sorry for. What was she doing there, by the way? I thought Mr Summerfield was on detention duty?

JOHNSON: He was. I think she's been trying to win him round to her way of thinking. You know what she's like.

MRS HEPWORTH: Miss Steadman is a very experienced and able teacher.

JOHNSON: That's more than can be said for Mr Summerfield –

MRS HEPWORTH: I don't really think this is the time or the place to discuss matters like that, Mr Johnson.

JOHNSON: I should never have put him on that detention duty, not with Blower in there. I should have known there'd be some kind of trouble.

MRS HEPWORTH: Not this, though.

(*The* FIRST POLICE OFFICER *approaches.*)

FIRST OFFICER: Excuse me, Mrs Hepworth. We've just had word from the hospital. The Turner boy's all right. It was just a small wound, nothing serious, no damage done.

MRS HEPWORTH: Thank goodness for that, at least.

JOHNSON: What are you going to do about all this, officer?

FIRST OFFICER: Well, sir, for the present, we feel that it's best just to wait for a while.

JOHNSON: Wait for what?

FIRST OFFICER: They're only kids, aren't they? And there's only three of them. One of our lads has been up and had a word with them through the door, told them what's what. We think they'll get fed up sooner or later.

JOHNSON: And what if they don't? Blower's got a knife, you know.

FIRST OFFICER: We're well aware of the situation, sir, and of the possible dangers. There are two officers waiting in the corridor. They're keeping an eye on things. It's all quiet in there at the moment.

JOHNSON: You still haven't said what you're going to do if they don't come out.

FIRST OFFICER: We have everything planned. We'll just wait for a while longer and see how things go. It's best to play these situations down, take things slowly.

MRS HEPWORTH: Yes. I think that's wise.

JOHNSON: Those kids. Three stupid kids causing all this trouble. If I could just get my hands on them –

MRS HEPWORTH: I think it's best if we let the police handle this in their own way. I'm sure they know what they're doing.

FIRST OFFICER: Thank you. Well, I'll just get along back to the car. I'll keep you informed of any further developments. (*He goes*)

MRS HEPWORTH: There's one thing I don't understand, and that's how Turner came to be in that room in the first place. He wasn't in detention, was he?

JOHNSON: No. I don't understand any of it. In all my years of teaching, I've never known anything like it. Kids think they can get away with anything today.

MRS HEPWORTH: It's all so distressing. If only I'd been here at the time. I had to go to that meeting. If I had been here, I'm sure that between us you and I could have handled it on our own, without the police having to be involved. I do not like having the police involved in school matters. It only increases the tension. (*Pause*) How long have they been up there now?

JOHNSON: Just over an hour.

MRS HEPWORTH: The longer it goes on, the worse it's going to get.

JOHNSON: It's that Blower. He's the cause of it all. A mental case, he is. I always knew he'd cause some big trouble some day. Still. It runs in the family.

MRS HEPWORTH: What do you mean?

JOHNSON: You know about his mother, don't you? She's been going in and out of mental homes for years.

MRS HEPWORTH: No . . . I didn't know that . . .

JOHNSON: It's no wonder he's like he is.

MRS HEPWORTH: I suppose the papers will get hold of it. They always do. It won't do the school's reputation any good. And just when we were beginning to get on top of things, just as we were making some headway.

JOHNSON: You never make any headway with that lot.

MRS HEPWORTH: You think that?

JOHNSON: For some of them, yes.

(*Pause.*)

MRS HEPWORTH: Then why do we bother at all?

(*Pause. Lights fade.*)

Scene 3 *The classroom.*

(*As before.* MANDY *is looking out of the window.*)

BLOWER: What's happening?

MANDY: Nothing.

BLOWER: Sure?

MANDY: Yeah. Hepworth and Johnson are still standing around, and there's a copper by the car.

MAKHAN: Just one copper?

MANDY: Just the one.

MAKHAN: There was three. Where's the other two?

BLOWER: Are they out in the corridor?

MAKHAN: I'll have a look. (*He looks out of the door window*) I can't see anybody.
BLOWER: They're out there, I bet. Just round the corner. Waiting for us. Well, they can wait.
MANDY: Till when?
BLOWER: Till we're ready.
MANDY: Ready for what?
BLOWER: What you keep asking me questions for, Mandy? I'm sick of it.
MANDY: I just wanna know what's gonna happen next?
BLOWER: Whatever we want to happen! We gotta tell them our terms yet.
MANDY: What terms? You keep on about these stupid terms. But we don't even know what they are. We ain't even talked about them.
BLOWER: What we want.
MANDY: What do we want, though?
BLOWER: Will you stop going on?
MANDY: We don't want anything, do we? We don't know what we want. We don't even know what were doing here!
BLOWER: Will you shurrup!
MAKHAN: Stop it, the two of you! It ain't no good arguing amongst ourselves.
NICK: She's right, though, isn't she? You know she's right. You don't know what you want.
BLOWER: Shurrup, Summerfield. Don't try throwing your weight about here.
SARAH: We're not throwing our weight about. How can we?
BLOWER: You'd like to.
SARAH: We're not all like that, you know. Some of us are better than others.
BLOWER: You're all the same. You. Summerfield. Johnson. You're all teachers.
SARAH: Some of us really do care. We do want to help you. We're on your side.
BLOWER: On our side! That's a laugh, that is.
SARAH: Mandy. You know I'm right.

135

MANDY: I dunno, miss. Perhaps you do try. How do I know? But if you do, it don't do much good. Nothing ever changes for us round here.

SARAH: It could do, if you'd just give us a chance –

NICK: Save your breath, Sarah. They don't want us to help them. They want us to be the enemy. Isn't that right? Because if we weren't, that would make this whole thing pointless. It is pointless, but they won't admit that. Or they can't. Because they're too thick to see it.

SARAH: Nick!

BLOWER: It's coming out now, ain't it?

NICK: That's all they are, thick kids who feel big because they've got a knife and a chance to push somebody around. That's all this is. Nothing more than that. It's just a bit of excitement in their boring lives.

MAKHAN: That ain't true. You know it ain't. You know what happened.

NICK: Thugs. That's all you are. Hooligans. You deserve all the punishment you get.

BLOWER: Just like Johnson.

NICK: I hope they put you away!

SARAH: Nick! Shut up!

MANDY: That's right, miss. Tell him to shut up! He's getting on my nerves.

BLOWER: If he don't, I'll use this on him. (*He holds up the knife*)

MAKHAN: No, Kev.

BLOWER: I'll shut him up.

MAKHAN: You won't. We ain't gonna hurt them.

MANDY: That's right, Kev. The knife's just to scare them with. We ain't gonna use it really.

BLOWER: It ain't up to you. It's my knife. If I want to use it, I will. (*To* NICK) Stand up! I said stand up!

(NICK *stands.*)

Go to the blackboard. Go on!

(NICK *crosses to the blackboard.*)

Get a piece of chalk and draw a circle on the board.
SARAH: What are you doing, Kevin?
BLOWER: Mind your own business. Draw that circle.

(NICK *does so.*)

Right. Now put your nose in the middle of it.
NICK: What?
BLOWER: You heard. Stand against the blackboard with your nose in the middle of that circle. Go on. Do it!
MAKHAN: Stop it, Kev.
BLOWER: I said do it!

(NICK *does so.* BLOWER *laughs.*)

NICK: What do I do now?
BLOWER: Nothing. Just stand there.
NICK: This is stupid.
BLOWER: Yeah. I know it is. Makes you feel really stupid, doesn't it?
MANDY: What's the point, Kev?
BLOWER: The point is there ain't no point. That's the point. It's a waste of time. It's stupid.
NICK: How long have I got to stand here for?
BLOWER: Till I tell you to move. I stood there for half an hour. Johnson made me do that once, when I was in the first year. That's when I decided I hated him, and all the other teachers.
SARAH: We've never done anything like that.
BLOWER: It don't matter. You will do some day. 'Cos you're all the same. You're all on the same side. When you come into the classroom, you go behind that big desk and we sit behind these little ones. When it's break, we have to go outside, but you go to the staffroom and have some tea or some coffee. You can push in the queue at lunchtime while we have to wait. That's the difference. That's the point.

(NICK *turns round.*)

I ain't told you to move.
NICK: I don't care. I'm not doing it any more.

BLOWER: Get back there.
NICK: No.
BLOWER: I'm telling you.
NICK: I'm going to sit down.
BLOWER: That's it, then!

(NICK *goes to sit.* BLOWER *steps forwards with the knife.* NICK *cries out in fear.* MANDY *grabs* BLOWER's *hand.*)

MANDY: No, Kev. You can't!

(*Pause.* NICK *sits. He starts to cry.*)

NICK: I hate you ... I hate you all ... I hate you ...

(*Pause.*)

SARAH: Proud of yourself, Kevin? Are you proud you've done that to him?

(*Pause.*)

MANDY: Miss Steadman ... Mr Summerfield ... I didn't ... I didn't want any of this ... I'm sorry ...
BLOWER: Whose side are you on, Mandy?
MANDY: Does there have to be sides? (*Pause*) I just wish all this was over with. I wish they'd come up and get us, or something. I'm tired. I just wanna go home and go to bed. I could sleep for hours.
BLOWER: We ain't giving up. Just let them try and get us. (*He runs to the window, opens it, and calls out*) We ain't giving up. You'll have to come and get us. Just come and try it. You hear?

(*Pause.*)

MAKHAN: You needn't have bothered, Kev. I got a feeling it won't be very long now.

(*He sits. Lights fade.*)

Act Two

SCENE 4 *Outside in the playground.*

(JOHNSON *and* MRS HEPWORTH *are waiting.*)

JOHNSON: It shouldn't be very much longer now.
MRS HEPWORTH: Thank goodness.
JOHNSON: I only hope Blower isn't idiot enough to use that knife before the police get to him.
MRS HEPWORTH: I don't think he will. I'm sure he won't.
JOHNSON: I wouldn't put anything past him.

(*Pause.*)

MRS HEPWORTH: You know, I can't help thinking that this is partly our fault.
JOHNSON: Us? What do you mean?
MRS HEPWORTH: Not you and I. All of us. It stands to reason in a sense. They are in our charge, they're our responsibility. It's our job to educate them, to mould them into good citizens of the future.
JOHNSON: There are some people you can never get through to.
MRS HEPWORTH: How old are they now? Sixteen. That means that, altogether, they've been at one school or another for eleven years. Eleven years. And this is the result. Something must be going wrong somewhere. We must be making some kind of mistakes. If you can't achieve something in eleven years ...
JOHNSON: We can't do everything. We're not miracle workers.
MRS HEPWORTH: I just wish I didn't feel so ... helpless ... so useless ...

(*The* FIRST POLICE OFFICER *approaches.*)

FIRST OFFICER: Mrs Hepworth. Everything's arranged. We feel the time's about ripe now. We'll have it all over with in a jiffy.
JOHNSON: Good. About time too.
FIRST OFFICER: One of my men tells me there's been some shouting. Seems they've started to argue amongst themselves. Getting too much for them now, I suppose. This is about the best time to go in, I should think.

MRS HEPWORTH: You will be careful, won't you?
FIRST OFFICER: We're always careful. Nobody will get hurt. Kids. They love to cause trouble. I blame society. Everyone's too soft with them.
JOHNSON: I couldn't agree more.
FIRST OFFICER: If you want my opinion, I think a quick clip round the ear at the right time can save all this kind of trouble. Stops things from building up. You want to nip things in the bud. Still –
JOHNSON: Look – (*He points upwards*)
MRS HEPWORTH: Isn't that Blower?
JOHNSON: Yes.
MRS HEPWORTH: What's he doing up there?
FIRST OFFICER: He seems to be shouting something.
JOHNSON: What is it?
MRS HEPWORTH: I can't make it out. I think you'd better get up there as quickly as you can.
FIRST OFFICER: You're right. We'd better get on with it. (*He goes*)
MRS HEPWORTH: He's stopped. I wonder what it was he was saying?
JOHNSON: It doesn't matter. Nothing important. Nothing worth listening to.

(*Lights fade.*)

SCENE 5 *The classroom.*

(MAKHAN *is looking out of the window.*)

MAKHAN: That copper's gone.
BLOWER: What?
MAKHAN: The one who was outside. He ain't there any more.
BLOWER: Where is he?
MAKHAN: How should I know?
BLOWER: Get by the table. And you, Mandy.
MANDY: What for?
BLOWER: They ain't gonna get in.
MANDY: We won't be able to stop them.
BLOWER: We can try. We can fight them.

Act Two

MANDY: I don't want to fight them.
BLOWER: Get against the table!
MANDY: No!
BLOWER: Mak. Will you tell her?
MAKHAN: I dunno, Kev. Maybe she's right. It ain't no good trying to fight the coppers. It'll just make everything worse.
BLOWER: You two! What are you? Chicken, or something?
MANDY: Yeah. I am. I am scared. I'm sick of all this. I just want to go home. I didn't even want this to happen. I didn't want to be no terrorist or anything like that. I like Miss Steadman and Mr Summerfield. I like them both. They're all right. We got the wrong ones here. They ain't never done us any harm.
BLOWER: They're the only ones we've got.
SARAH: Listen. Why don't you give up?
BLOWER: Don't start on that again.
SARAH: You haven't got much time. The police will be in here soon. You know you can't fight them. If you give up before they come in, it will show you never meant any harm. It'll go in your favour.
MAKHAN: That's sense, Kev. It's all over now anyway. There ain't much more we can do.
BLOWER: No!
MAKHAN: This was all a mistake anyway. An accident. We tried to do something with it, but it went wrong. The only chance we got now is to go out, show them we ain't just hooligans and thugs. Maybe they'll listen to us then.
BLOWER: You just ain't got any guts. I'm the only one with guts here.
SARAH: I'll side with you. I'll speak with you. I promise. I'll explain how it happened.
BLOWER: She's just creeping.
SARAH: No, I'm not.
MANDY: Why don't you listen to her, Kev? She's always been all right with us before.
SARAH: I'll tell them about Turner, about last night, how he came in and started all this. I've been trying to get something done about him and his kind for a long time. This'll be our chance.

MAKHAN: And will you tell them about Johnson as well?
SARAH: Johnson?
MAKHAN: Yeah. Tell them what he's like. How he slapped Kev round the head. How he's always pushing us around.
SARAH: All right, yes, I will.
BLOWER: Don't believe her. She's just saying that now to get us to give up. She won't do it when the time comes.
SARAH: Yes, I will. I promise. I understand you –
BLOWER: No, you don't. How can you? You don't live on our estate, you weren't born on this dump. You ain't gotta grow up here, and grow old here, and die here. You don't know what it's like. People look at you like you come from another planet if you tell them you come from this estate. They treat you like a leper. Nobody does anything for you. You know my grandad's pigeons? You know what happened to them? He took a pride in them pigeons, he loved them, we both did. Then one night somebody broke into the shed and killed them. Broke their necks. Scattered their bodies all over the floor. He broke down when he found them. They was all he lived for. So he went to the police and told them, but they didn't do anything about it, because he come from round here, and that kind of thing's always happening round here, so it don't matter. He was never the same after that. That's why he gave up. And that's why you'll never understand. Because you don't live round here, and them things never happened to you.
SARAH: Just give me a chance, trust me –
NICK: He doesn't want to. He doesn't want to give up.
BLOWER: Right.
NICK: This is his moment of glory. He doesn't want to give that up. He wants to go down fighting, don't you?
SARAH: Shut up, Nick.
NICK: He's got that knife and he wants to use it. He's been dying to, haven't you? He's got the taste of blood.
BLOWER: Shut your trap.

(NICK *stands*.)

NICK: Come on, then, Blower. Come on. Use it. I'm here.

MAKHAN: Sit down.
NICK: Use it on me. I'm waiting. I won't be able to stop you. You know that.
MANDY: Make him shut up, somebody.
SARAH: Nick, you're ruining everything.
NICK: I'm weak. I can't control you. I've never been able to stop you doing anything before, have I? Why don't you use it?
BLOWER: If you don't keep away from me, I will.
NICK: No more threats, Blower. Use it. Use it!
BLOWER: Keep back!
NICK: Chicken, are you?
BLOWER: No, I ain't! (*He attacks* NICK. *He does not use the knife, but hits him and knocks him down. He starts to kick him*) I'll show you ... I'll teach you ...
SARAH: No, don't ...
MANDY: Kev, stop it ...
MAKHAN: Get off him, Kev ...
MANDY: Get his knife before he uses it.

(MAKHAN *grabs the knife off* BLOWER. BLOWER *turns on him.* SARAH *kneels by* NICK.)

BLOWER: Give me that knife.
MAKHAN: No, Kev.
BLOWER: It's mine!
MAKHAN: It's for your own good.
BLOWER: Give me my knife, wog!

(*Pause.*)

MAKHAN: You'll have to come and get it from me.

(MANDY *looks out of the door window.*)

MANDY: The coppers are coming along the corridor!
MAKHAN: Get the desk away from the door.

(MANDY *moves the desk.*)

BLOWER: Cowards!
MANDY: It's the best thing.

MAKHAN: Remember what you said, miss.
SARAH: I will.
BLOWER: You lot can give up, but I ain't. (*He climbs onto the window ledge*) Nobody's gonna get me.
SARAH: Kevin, get down!

(*The door bursts open. Three* POLICE OFFICERS *rush in.*)

FIRST OFFICER: Get him with the knife. And the girl.

(MANDY *screams. The* SECOND POLICE OFFICER *grabs* MAKHAN.)

SECOND OFFICER: Come here.
MAKHAN: All right, you can have the knife. I ain't fighting.
MANDY: Nor me. Leave me alone.
THIRD OFFICER: Are you two all right, miss?
SARAH: Yes, we're fine. Really.
FIRST OFFICER: What about the one at the window?

(NICK *stands.*)

NICK: I'll get him.

(*He runs at the window and grabs at* BLOWER. *There is a short struggle.* BLOWER *cries out and falls out of the window.*)

(*All fall silent. Pause.* NICK *looks down out of the window.*)

(*Lights fade to blackout.*)

SCENE 6   MRS HEPWORTH's *study.*

(MRS HEPWORTH *shows* SARAH *in.*)

MRS HEPWORTH: Sit down, Sarah.

(*They both sit.*)

Would you like a cup of tea?
SARAH: No, thank you.

(*Pause.*)

Act Two

MRS HEPWORTH: It's good to see you again. I trust you're fully recovered now?

SARAH: Oh, yes.

MRS HEPWORTH: It must have been a very trying ordeal for you.

SARAH: Of course.

MRS HEPWORTH: And for us all, in a way. The whole school has suffered.

SARAH: I can imagine.

MRS HEPWORTH: That first week after the ... incident. Things were very fraught. Our whole routine was upset. And you know how this kind of thing unsettles the children. We had some very difficult times. And then there was the police coming in, and having to see parents, and trying to keep the press at bay. It seemed like a nightmare. But things appear to be getting back to normal again, thank goodness.

SARAH: Yes. When I came in, just now, it seemed as if nothing at all had happened. Everything was going on as usual.

MRS HEPWORTH: It's important that we try to forget these things as soon as possible, I think. I'm relieved that Blower was not hurt as badly as he might have been. He was a very lucky boy. I've been to see him.

SARAH: Have you?

MRS HEPWORTH: Of course. It was my duty. Also, I wanted to talk to him. I wanted to try and find out – why they did it. What they wanted to achieve. I still don't understand, you see.

SARAH: What did he say?

MRS HEPWORTH: Something rather odd, actually. He said to ask you. He said you'd tell me. (*Pause*) Does that make any sense to you?

(SARAH *says nothing.*)

I thought not. Just one of his clever answers. Or what he thinks is clever.

SARAH: I think ... they wanted us to listen to them.

MRS HEPWORTH: Listen to them?

SARAH: To what they had to say.

MRS HEPWORTH: But we do listen to them. I pride myself on

having a very caring staff here, as you well know, Sarah. Teachers who will and do listen to children's problems. We have an excellent pastoral system here, we know what problems are going to arise before they do –

SARAH: We didn't know about this one, did we? (*Pause*) I'm sorry.

MRS HEPWORTH: That's quite all right. I understand how the whole incident must have upset you. I am very glad that you are coming back to us, though. I was a little worried that you might take Mr Summerfield's course of action and resign. Have you seen him at all?

SARAH: No, I haven't.

MRS HEPWORTH: It's a great pity. I couldn't dissuade him. He did show some promise. I know he had one or two problems but, after all, this was his probationary year.

SARAH: He couldn't do anything else but resign, could he? I mean. He pushed Blower.

MRS HEPWORTH: I beg your pardon?

SARAH: He pushed Blower out of the window.

(*Pause.*)

MRS HEPWORTH: I'm afraid you're mistaken, Sarah. Blower fell.

SARAH: I was there. I saw it. Nick pushed Blower.

MRS HEPWORTH: Mr Summerfield was trying to get Blower down from the window. Blower struggled, and in the course of that struggle, he fell.

SARAH: I see. That's the official line, is it?

MRS HEPWORTH: It's the truth.

SARAH: We're closing ranks, protecting our own. Can't let any harm come to the profession, can we? If anything goes wrong, we have to blame it all on the kids ...

MRS HEPWORTH: I think that these three particular children can take a large share of the blame. They have a lot to answer for.

SARAH: Mrs Hepworth, please believe me. I saw it. I saw Nick go to the window and push Blower out. I'm not making it up. He's resigned. Can't we just admit that? That he did push him?

MRS HEPWORTH: We can't admit anything we're not sure of. There was a lot of confusion in that classroom. The police say

Act Two

that everything happened very quickly. I mean, are you absolutely certain that what you say happened?

SARAH: I thought ... yes ... I don't know ...

MRS HEPWORTH: You see? Now, would you jeopardise the whole standing of our profession for something you're not sure of? There's a lot that we can achieve at this school for these children, a lot that can be done. There's much that you can do yourself. Surely you don't want to throw all that away? Because of something you thought might have happened? It's all over now, Sarah, it's in the past. It's best to try and forget about it, and look to the future.

SARAH: Yes. Yes. I suppose you're right.

MRS HEPWORTH: Of course.

SARAH: There was something I had to say.

MRS HEPWORTH: What?

SARAH: Something ... (*Pause*) It doesn't matter. I'm sorry. I think I'm still feeling a bit upset.

MRS HEPWORTH: That's quite natural. But once you're back at school, once you're doing your job again you'll find that everything will be all right again. (*She stands*) Now. I'll have the secretary make you a nice hot cup of tea. You'll feel much better after that.

(*She goes out. SARAH sits alone. Lights to blackout.*)

Support and Resources

Challenges
Four plays by Grazyna Monvid from ITV's 'Starting Out' series: 'Escapes', 'To Be Or Not To Be', 'Prejudice' and 'Taken On Trust'.

Choices
A companion volume of four plays by Grazyna Monvid from the same series: 'Arrangements', 'As Good As You Get', 'All Right For Some' and 'Life and Death'.

Both of these collections contain a variety of approaches to work in the classroom, much of which touches issues raised in the present collection. They are published by Heinemann Educational, 1986, in the Floodlights series.

The English Curriculum: Race
An excellent support for the individual teacher, and for the English Department. Available from the English Centre, Sutherland Street, London SW1.

Issues and Resources
An excellent handbook and resource list. Available from AFFOR (All Faiths for One Race), 173 Lozells Road, Lozells, Birmingham B19 1RN.

Viewpoint
Andrew Bethall, Cambridge University Press, 1979. A supportive collection of teaching strategies aimed at challenging stereotyping.

Some People Will Believe Anything: Myths and Facts about Immigration and Race Relations
A straightforward one-page pamphlet useful to have at hand during discussion. Available from the Commission for Racial Equality, Eliot House, 10–12 Allington Street, London SW1E 5EH (01-828 7022).

Teaching Controversial Issues
Robert Stradling, Michael Noctor and Bridget Baines, Edward Arnold, 1984.

This is, by necessity, a brief list. I would recommend that teachers contact their local multi-cultural support unit (via the LEA) for further advice and resource lists.

www.ingramcontent.com/pod-product-compliance
Ingram Content Group UK Ltd.
Pitfield, Milton Keynes, MK11 3LW, UK
UKHW021843210426
5322IPUK00022B/430